PICKING UP THE PIECES

PICKING UP THE PIECES

Patricia M. Lowther

Book Guild Publishing
Sussex, England

First published in Great Britain in 2009 by
The Book Guild
Pavilion View
19 New Road
Brighton, BN1 1UF

Typesetting in Times by
Keyboard Services, Luton, Bedfordshire

Printed in Great Britain by
CPI Antony Rowe

A catalogue record for this book is available from
The British Library

ISBN 978 1 84624 358 5

For Anne, Paul, Christopher and Cathleen,
and, most of all, for Alex –
17.3.1926–4.1.2009

Preface

In 1954 my husband and I emigrated to South Africa with our two children. Subsequently we had two more children but sadly my husband died when my youngest little girl was 14 months old. During our time there we had become Salvation Army Officers running various social centres, but after his death there seemed to be no place for me and my children.

After sticking it out for a few years, I made the decision to bring my family back to England. Although almost penniless, I started the long task of making a life for us all in a country which, although familiar to me, was very different from the place where my children had grown up.

This is the story of how life turned out for us all in the England of the late sixties and onwards.

Pat Lowther

1

As the plane took off from Jan Smuts airport in Johannesburg, I gazed out to take a last look at the far-flung, sunburnt veldt. In the fading light the horizon was cloaked in the smoky haze of the fires in the townships, but I was leaving this beautiful and vibrant country after fourteen years to return to make a life for myself and my family back in England. My two elder children, who had been born in England and who had come to South Africa with my husband and me fourteen years ago, had already left and were with my aunt in Newcastle. The two younger children, both born out here in South Africa, were now travelling with me to an uncertain future back in the country I used to call 'home'.

Settling the children down for the long journey ahead, I indulged in a few moments of regret at how things had turned out. The missed opportunities, then the life that had seemed to stretch out forever, before it was so tragically snatched away on Ron's death, followed by the gradual realisation that not only was there no future for me with the Salvation Army, but also that I was an embarrassment as a widow with four children to consider.

But this was not the time for regrets, I had made my decision and despite the difficulties I had scraped our air fares together. Now I must look to the future for myself and for my children. Deep down I was confident that I would be able, one way or the other, to provide for us all and once more to carve out a new life in what had become a foreign country to me, and which for the children would be an entirely new experience. How we would cope was still to be seen, but for now I concentrated on the immediate task ahead.

Trek Airways was a recently opened airline which was being run if not on a shoestring, certainly without any frills. At that time, in January 1968, flights from South Africa to Europe were no longer allowed to use the direct route via Nairobi which I had travelled two years before on my visit to Newcastle with my youngest child Cathleen. We would have to take a roundabout route to the west avoiding the central African States. Our first stop was to be Luanda in Angola where we would have to leave the plane while it was refuelled. Before we landed we were given a strict warning that we should not attempt to take any photos nor leave the airport lounge as the situation was very sensitive due to the political situation at that time. So, holding Christopher and Cathleen close to me, I walked with the other passengers across the hot tarmac to where the airport buildings shimmered in the heat and tried not to look to the right where fighter planes were clustered around a hangar on the far side of the airport.

We were ushered through double doors into the large, bare waiting area with few chairs and no facilities, while ranged around the balcony above us were black soldiers in army fatigues carrying what I assumed were AK 47s. They seemed to sense our apprehension and laughed and joked together as they looked down on us. It seemed best to try to ignore them and gaze fixedly out of the terminal doors where we could see our plane being refuelled. The waiting couldn't end soon enough for us and we thankfully trooped back across the tarmac and reboarded our plane.

The seemingly interminable journey went on through the night and when we woke we were flying across the desert sands which undulated beneath us. Eventually we reached our next destination, Malta, where we had been told we would be spending the day and the coming night before setting off again the next day for Luxemburg. A bus picked us up and drove us through the streets of what I assumed was Valetta, although I didn't really know. We skirted the side of a wide bay and arrived at the doors of the Malta Hilton. This was a bit of a surprise, but I could only assume that as the hotel had just been completed the airline had been able to do a deal, as this was January with few, if any, tourists, and the newly employed staff needed people on whom to practise their roles. So, somewhat overawed, we checked in and, clutching our overnight bags, were shown to our room.

These were the early days of tourist hotels and we gaped at the unexpected luxury of our accommodation. On one side of the entrance hall was a range of wardrobes while on the other was a beautiful marble bathroom with plenty of fluffy towels, shampoos and shower gels; in the room itself werc two enormous single beds and a smaller bed for three and a half-year-old Cathleen. After our gruelling flight it felt like heaven and we settled in before joining our party for a belated breakfast cum lunch. Our group were the only guests, and after we had eaten I made enquiries at the desk and was directed outside the hotel to a rank of horse-drawn carriages. The air was brisk and there had been an early fall of rain so that the streets and pavements glistened in the sun. The carriage we chose took us at a dignified pace along the road bordering the small bay while above us were rank upon rank of small houses painted in pastel colours and all with TV antennae sticking out above their flat roofs. They reminded me of nothing more than a set of cave dwellings set into the hillside. Otherwise the landscape seemed bare with very little vegetation to speak of and we soon returned to the hotel. After a short rest we gathered again for an evening meal which we all enjoyed and then returned to our room to prepare for the night.

The room had wide glass doors leading onto a small

3

balcony and, as our floor was actually lower than the main reception and dining areas, below us was rough scrubland beyond which we could just make out the sea. Far out we could see the lights of several ships. To our amazement, from the area beside the sea, a fantastic firework display began with rockets, shooting stars and great blossoming shimmers of light in all the colours of the rainbow. The children and I stood entranced throughout the whole show, and after it was all over we settled down for the night and a well-earned sleep.

Next morning, after an early call, we made good use of the shower and bathroom facilities before we went upstairs to the dining room and enjoyed a substantial breakfast. There we found out that the firework display had been for the benefit of the American fleet which had anchored off the island the previous night, the Hilton chain being, of course, an American company. We boarded our bus and were taken back to the airport and in brilliant sunshine took off on the flight to Luxemburg. The sight of the mountain ranges below us was breathtaking with their blankets of snow, but soon the skies began to cloud over. As we descended we drifted in and out of the clouds with the occasional sight of mountain tops, too close, in my opinion, for comfort, until at last we taxied down the runway and disembarked at Luxemburg for yet another change of plane. The air terminal here seemed deserted, rather like a huge hangar, but at one end it seemed that all the passengers were congregating at some sort of counter. Curious, I wandered over, only to find everyone buying cigarettes and whisky. Having neither the money nor the inclination to make such purchases I returned to our seats somewhat puzzled, but of course I was later to be introduced to the vagaries of the UK tax system and its various loopholes.

Once more we set off in another plane and this time we were set down at Gatwick where we bade farewell to Trek Airways, which although rough and ready had served us well. We now had to get to Heathrow Airport to catch a plane to Newcastle Airport and, as advised by the travel agent before we left South Africa, we went to the front of the terminal where we caught a bus which would take us there.

At the time we left South Africa television had still not arrived, as the Nationalist Government were suspicious of its influence upon the people and anyway, who had ever heard of any programmes being made in Afrikaans? Rumours of its delights had reached us from Rhodesia, however, and for Christopher one of the highlights of coming to England was to see television. Consequently, as the bus took us through small town high streets on its way to Heathrow, he had his nose glued to the bus window trying to look into the windows of the TV shops.

At Heathrow we had to wait a while for our flight but eventually we were called up first to be seated before the rest of the passengers, as I was travelling alone with the two children, and we set off on the final leg of our gruelling trip.

I thought back over the fourteen years since I had left England with my husband Ron and our two eldest children, Anne and Paul. Later Christopher was born, and nine years after that, somewhat unexpectedly, Cathleen had arrived. I had gone to South Africa with such high hopes for my husband and me. His elder sister Margery and her husband, Bram Jeavons, had been sent out there by the Salvation Army; Bram was the Appeals Organiser. Ron's parents, to everyone's surprise, had followed a year later and after I had had a second bout of TB we too had sold up and gone to live in the rarefied air of the High Veldt. I had undergone a complete cure, but sadly Ron had become an alcoholic, causing much anguish and many problems for us all. And then, miraculously, he had once more given his life to God at a Salvation Army meeting, and overnight ceased his drinking. He was accepted back as an Army Officer and, as

5

both husband and wife had to be trained, I had spent two years at the Army's Training College and had been commissioned as a Salvation Army Officer as well.

Together we ran various Army institutions until finally, while running the Johannesburg Men's Home, my husband suffered a second and fatal attack of coronary thrombosis. I was transferred with the children, first of all to the Girl's Home, and then to be in charge of the Young Women's Hostel in the city. After it was sold I went to the Training College as an assistant, but now I was returning to the UK for good. It seemed to me that there was no longer a place for me in South Africa.

Again I fell to wondering what the future would hold for us all. I was returning virtually penniless apart from £50 in the Newcastle Building Society which my great-aunt Allie had given me. During her lifetime she had opened savings accounts for each one of her nieces and nephews, and whenever she visited Newcastle she would deposit a pound in each account until the sum of £50 was reached, at which point she sent the relevant pass book to each of us. As a good weekly wage at that time was in the region of £10 this was a sum not to be sniffed at, and for me it was all that stood between me and poverty. Initially we were to stay with Auntie Ethel, my father's unmarried sister who had been my guardian after his accidental death, but as I had left South Africa under my own steam I couldn't expect the Salvation Army to consider helping me, plus it had already been made fairly clear to me that a widow with four children was something of a liability.

Anne had had her sixteenth birthday the previous June and Paul was fifteen. I had hopes that Paul might be taken on as an apprentice by the Air Force so that he could be trained for a career which would stand him in good stead. Anne I wasn't so sure about. I knew she had a high IQ but it had proved hard to encourage her to take her school studies seriously and in addition she found it difficult, in fact impossible, to accept any sort of instructions, but was blithely convinced that she knew it all. This had been demonstrated when they had returned to the UK ahead of me. I had told them both that when they arrived at Gatwick they should proceed to the airport entrance where a bus would take them to Heathrow for a reasonable sum, as indeed we had just done ourselves. A few days after they had left I received a letter from them telling me how exciting it had been to see central London! To my dismay, I knew that things had gone wrong.

I later learned that, confused by the crowded airport, they had gone to an enquiry desk where they were told there was no such bus and were directed to the trains. Dragging their bulging suitcases with them they had reached central London and made their way to the BA offices, who kindly loaded them into a bus for Heathrow. By the time they got there their plane connection to Newcastle was long gone, but they were fortunate enough to be put on a plane being repositioned in Newcastle for the next day's flight. Arriving eventually at Newcastle Airport, they discovered that my cousin Bill, who had volunteered to meet them, had given up and gone home, as he had been told that the last plane of the day had arrived and there was still no sign of them. So they got a taxi to my aunt's home at Woodburn, arriving at some time in the early hours. I couldn't imagine how worried she must have been. In those days, before the rapid communication we now take for granted, she had been unable to contact me, so I had been spared the worry that she must have felt.

All of this boded ill for our future prospects, but I refused to let it worry me. I would just have to meet our difficulties one at a time and deal with things as and when they arose. I would have to find a school for Christopher who at just turned twelve would qualify for the local comprehensive. Cathleen would be four in another few months.

At last the plane approached Newcastle and I was once more looking down on the sweep of the Tyne valley, but this time, unlike my arrival two years ago on a fact-finding visit, we landed at the newly built airport, where my cousin Bill was waiting for us.

Five years younger than me, Bill was the only son of my father's younger brother Stan, with whom my father had been in business before his untimely death at the age of 35. My aunt later remarried and had two daughters, but as youngsters Bill and I had shared many adventures when sledging or youth hostelling and hiking across the moors. He remained an ardent bird fancier and spent many happy times in the north of Scotland helping to ring birds and observing their habits.

We had struck up a correspondence during my final years in South Africa. He and his wife Audrey were the parents of Jacqueline, and their second child was on the way.

Thankfully, we loaded ourselves and our luggage into Bill's car and drove off towards Heaton and our destination. Auntie Ethel was waiting to welcome us but Christopher, on tenterhooks to see his first television set, barely said hello before he darted into the sitting room to stand transfixed in front of 'the box'.

Woodburn was an old stone-built farmhouse set down on the edge of Armstrong Park and in a deep valley which cut its way between the suburbs of Heaton and Jesmond. On the other side of the road stretched Jesmond Dene with its woods and rhododendron-carpeted sides. The road that cut through the valley to reach the city was called Benton Bank where now the buses thundered up and down instead of the trams of my youth. Woodburn had been bought by my grandfather in 1935. He, my grandmother and their two unmarried daughters, Ethel and Maryon, lived there, while on the land next door my father and his brother Stan and wife Nancy built a pair of semi-detached houses. It was in our house, 'Parkside', that my mother died of TB at the age of 28. I was five and we were looked after by our maid Florence until the war broke out and I was evacuated. When I returned three years later, my father, having let our house, was living in Woodburn; my grandparents had both died and the house had been left to Auntie Ethel, with Auntie Maryon still in situ. She later bought St Mary's Mount, a large house at the Jesmond end of Armstrong Bridge. The land stretched all the way down the hill to the stream at the bottom and provided her with space for the dogs she bred in the stables under the bridge.

Woodburn was not a large house, with two good-sized rooms on either side of the central hallway and at the rear a bathroom, kitchen and a room which used to be 'the office' when my father had his business, but which was now used by Auntie Ethel as a kitchen. She had let what used to be the drawing room as a bed-sitter to two girls working at 'The Ministry' as the Central Office of the Department of Health and Social Security was known locally. They had the sole use of the kitchen, while the bathroom and toilet facilities were shared. Upstairs there were three bedrooms, one large one over the sitting room and two smaller ones made out of the space above the drawing room, so it was a bit of a squeeze and we were very lucky that Ethel was willing to take us in. It was an awful upheaval for her in her spinster status, where for years she had been on her own. Suddenly she was inundated with a young family and it was never going to be easy.

One of my first tasks was to go to the nearest Social Security Office to sort out my widow's pension and to see if it would be increased now that the children were in the UK as, while living in South Africa, I only received a pension for myself. I found my way to the office which was in a

9

temporary sort of wooden building in a road just off Stratford Villas. There were no problems in changing over the previous payments which used to come to me in South Africa in the form of money orders once a month, but now I would be given an order book and also receive money for Christopher and Cathleen. I would have to wait for six months before I received any Family Allowance for the children, and it would only be for one child as the eldest child did not qualify at that time. All this was explained to me and in the course of time I received my order book for a reduced Widowed Mother's Allowance.

Additionally, I had been given some Post War Credit certificates as part of my father's estate. This was a war-time scheme which took money from employees to use in the war effort to be paid back at some future date. As my father's heir, and as I was now widowed, I was entitled to claim the money back. I can't remember now how much I got, but the money was badly needed to buy us all warm winter clothing.

Paul had gone along to the recruiting office of the Air Force, but after interviewing him they decided that his South African educational qualifications were not sufficient. So before I arrived Auntie Ethel had taken him to the Employment Exchange and he had been given a job with the Co-op working on their mobile shop. Anne had got a job in an office as a filing clerk and tea maker, so for the moment we were reasonably stable. I took Chris to the local school and he started there almost immediately. Poor lad, we had changed to decimal currency a few years before we left South Africa, but England still used pounds, shillings and pence. In order to do his maths he would convert it all into decimals and then change it back after he had done the calculation. It would be a year or two before decimalisation arrived in the UK. When it did, I couldn't believe how stupidly it was done. Instead of using a ten shilling note as one unit and therefore making a shilling into ten pence, there was this urge to cling to the pound and instead *two* shillings became ten pence. Inevitably, the change-over produced a surge in inflation as retailers rounded up all their prices.

I had heard that the primary school at the end of Benton Road had a nursery class, so I went up to see the headmistress. She explained that the class had been started largely for the benefit of the children of teachers, but that they were open to other parents who could demonstrate a need. Obviously I fitted the criteria and she agreed that Cathleen could start there. I explained that Cathleen was having some problems and what the background was to our circumstances.

Cathleen had been born while Ron and I had been in charge of the Young Men's Hostel in Braamfontein, a suburb just on the edge of the city of Johannesburg. Her arrival had been a bit of a surprise as at that time our youngest child, Christopher, was nine years old. In addition, I was in my second and final year of training at the Salvation Army Training College for three days a week, while helping to run the hostel during the remaining days. Once the surprise had faded, we were only too happy to welcome another child into our family and were especially delighted when it turned out to be a girl. By the standards of that day, at 34 I was an 'older' mother but the birth went well, although a few months later I had to have a hysterectomy due to problems with my cervix.

After I was commissioned as a fully fledged Salvation Army Officer we were put in charge of the Men's Home in downtown Johannesburg and it was there, when Cathleen was 14 months old, that my husband died. Up until then Cathleen had been developing nicely, but in a panic move I was sent with the children to work at the Girl's Home where I was the only one who could drive and where I worked from the early hours of the morning until late at night, so that essentially Cathleen lost both mother and father.

When it became obvious that the situation was untenable, I was put in charge of the Young Women's Hostel in the centre of Johannesburg, which I ran until it was sold, after which I went to the Training College as a training officer. So in all that time I rarely had the opportunity to spend time with Cathleen, as she was cared for by my faithful Zulu nanny, Toni. Now we were back in England, and as I attempted to carve a more normal life out for my children and myself, it was obvious that that period had taken its toll and that at four years of age Cathleen had many developmental problems.

The headmistress was appalled at our experiences and said that she would do all she could to help Cathleen, who at that time was hardly talking at all. Meanwhile I made an appointment with the local GP who had a surgery in a large Victorian house at the bottom of Heaton Road. On entering his consulting room it was barely possible to make him out through the clouds of cigarette smoke. As he talked, he was never without a lit cigarette closely to hand. He briefly examined Cathleen and then said he would refer her to the Children's Department at the RVI, the Royal Victoria Infirmary just off the Haymarket in town. We duly went there, where her hearing was tested and we were interviewed, but no conclusions were reached and all in all it was a wasted effort. I knew something was wrong with her, but it seemed likely that if there was no medical problem, there would be little that could be done.

Auntie Ethel had had some unspecified heart problems. She regularly walked through Armstrong Park to the surgery of the doctor she attended on Heaton Park Road, a not inconsiderable distance. There she would be given a repeat prescription. Her doctor had not seen her or laid a stethoscope upon her for many a long year. I tried to persuade her to change to a doctor nearer to home and also to make an appointment for a more up-to-date examination, but she quietly declined.

Soon after we had settled in, I took us all to the nearest

Salvation Army Corps which was at the bottom of Westgate Road at the far end of the city. There we were made very welcome as the family of my brother-in-law, Bram Jeavons, Margery's husband, were life-long members of that Corps. There had been four children in the Jeavons family. Their parents had been Army Officers and they had retired to a large Edwardian house they owned just off the West Road beyond the General Hospital. Bram was the eldest, with two brothers, Cyril and Bernard and a younger sister Ruby. Cyril and his wife Dorothy owned shops in Newcastle selling musical instruments, and they had a lovely home out beyond Ponteland near to where the new airport had been built. Bernard was a bit of an odd character. He had been in the army during the war when he met a Dutch lady whom he married. He brought her back to England where she bore a son, but when he treated her so badly that she returned to live in Holland he refused to let her have their son, and the two lived together in a house on an estate in the West End.

Ruby had worked as secretary to a surgeon by the name of Collingwood-Stewart who had been a consultant at the General Hospital where I trained. When his wife died he married Ruby, who by now had had her brothers' share of the family home given to her. There they lived until he died a few years later leaving Ruby to reign as the noted Mrs Collingwood-Stewart, wielding influence on various committees and coming into her glory on the annual Trafalgar Day celebrations, her husband having been a descendant of the Collingwood who fought with Nelson.

So, feeling like a poor relation, I was taken on by this illustrious family and invited to sit with Ruby at the meetings. I liked Dorothy and Cyril and was invited to their home, but Auntie Ethel was a bit put out that they didn't invite her too. The next invitation was to a Tupperware Party, which I politely declined, having neither the money nor the inclination to buy Tupperware, then all the rage. Ruby, however, used her influence to bring an Army Officer to meet me who was in charge of a lot of the Army's social work. The outcome of that was an invitation to take up an appointment to work in a children's home somewhere in the south of England. After giving it some thought I declined as I couldn't face uprooting the children again. Meanwhile the Army in South Africa refunded my air fare from Johannesburg, but only for me not the children, so I put it in the savings account opened for me by Auntie Allie.

The girls who had rented the bed-sitter decided to leave as they had had a big win on the Premium Bonds and were returning to Ireland to care for their families. Knowing that Auntie would need the money, I asked if she would let it to me plus one of the bedrooms. By then I think she had had enough of us all, and she said no. There was some talk of them lending me the money to buy a flat or small house, but at that time I had no income. I went to the council to enquire about a council house and was invited to fill in all the forms, but they said that despite my need it could be over a year before anything would be available.

Then Louie came on the scene. His mother had been the midwife who delivered me and he and his brother had been regular visitors at my grandparents' house when they had been little boys, while their mother, a widow, had been out working. Louie was a Catholic with a large family, now all grown up or in their teens and was separated from his wife who had left him after buying, on the quiet, a house in the next street. He was always welcomed by Ethel and Maryon, and I myself had known him off and on since I was quite young.

I realised I would have to do something to earn some money. I had officially been given a year's leave of absence from the Army, unpaid of course, so that when I saw an advert for part-time nursing staff at St Nicholas' Hospital, a huge old-fashioned mental hospital, I applied for a job there,

14

giving as my referees Ruby and my father's old friend Archie Morrison, who was the manager of the Newcastle Building Society. I went for my interview and in no time at all was collecting my uniform and being introduced to the hospital.

It was awkwardly situated for me with no direct public transport. When I saw an advert for a second-hand bicycle, I bought it and used to cycle each morning along the narrow road running along the top of the valley of Jesmond Dene, often startling young rabbits in the pre-dawn light as I crept silently up on them.

St Nicholas' Hospital was the archetypal Victorian lunatic asylum set in enormous grounds which at one time had been farmed by the male inmates to provide fresh produce for the hospital. The buildings were made of solid stone, two-storeyed, with high narrow windows, and stretched along the whole length of the extensive grounds. The end nearest the gates contained the male patients cared for by male nurses, while the female end was run by the female staff. There were miles of long corridors with spurs leading off for the various wards and half-way down the main one was the staff dining room. Lunch break was half an hour, so that by the time I had walked down the corridor to the restaurant, queued for my food and gulped it down, it was a race to get back to the ward on time.

I soon discovered that the majority of the patients were old people who had been sent there after becoming senile and confused. Some, however, had spent most of their adult lives there, either because they had suffered from epilepsy which had now subsided, or because they had given birth to illegitimate children at the beginning of the century. Now in their seventies and eighties, they were so institutionalised that it would have been impossible for them to live outside these unlovely walls.

Along with my overalls, I was issued with a key which unlocked the main door to the ward to which I was assigned.

The first room on entering was a large dining area with a kitchen behind it. Further along the passage was the day room on the left with store rooms on the right. A door further along on the right led up a few steps to the bathrooms. These were large bare rooms with three baths placed so that they could be accessed on all sides. There the patients would be taken in turn to be bathed without any ceremony or privacy. The bedrooms were at the end with a dozen beds in each room.

The first task each morning was to get the women out of bed. Many had soiled themselves during the night. After cleaning and dressing everybody, we would serve breakfast from the heated trolley brought in by the porters. Many needed help with their feeding. After all had been cleared away, the sister would dole out the morning's drugs, mostly, as far as I could see, meant to keep them in a state of torpor. They were then shepherded into the day room, settled into the comfortable chairs and the television set turned on, but few took any interest in the flickering screen. We would talk to those who were more alert and keep an eye open for any puddles which formed under the chairs, the signal for a change of clothing.

I worked from 7 am to 2 pm for three days a week, but often I would be asked to work an extra shift when the hospital was short-staffed. It was hard work and not very pleasant; I always felt that I took the smell of it away with me on my clothes.

In a newer building near the gates there was an acute ward where emergency patients could be treated. There were two padded cells which, with the onset of newer drugs, were never needed for any length of time. They also had a mother and baby facility for treating acute post-natal depression and a set-up for administering electric shock therapy, which was still much in vogue at that time. As it was known that I had had general nursing training, I was selected to accompany some of the patients at our end of the hospital down to this place and to assist with the therapy. It was done almost on a conveyor-belt system. The patients would be put on a trolley and lined up in the waiting room where they would be given an injection to calm them down. They were then wheeled into the therapy room where anaesthetic was given and then an injection of curare to relax all the muscles. This had to be done otherwise the contortions produced by the electric impulses might result in broken limbs, but it also meant that the anaesthetist had to monitor the patient's breathing as normal respiration ceased due to the curare. The electrodes were then attached to the patient's head and the requisite number of shocks passed through the brain. The antidote to the curare was then given and, when round from the anaesthetic, the patient was taken into the room on the other side and put into a bed to recover. Once completely round from the anaesthetic they would be taken back to the ward, but usually remained fairly comatose for the rest of the day. This treatment was supposed to cure patients of depression and other acute forms of mental illness, but most of the patients that I took down from our end of the hospital didn't seem to me to have been helped.

After working there for some time, I was being asked to do so many extra shifts that I thought I may as well go full time and earn the extra money. In addition I could take up my training once more. As I had already passed some of my nursing exams, I would only have to train for a further year and that would open up some sort of a career structure for me. So I applied and was accepted into the next batch of trainees. We attended lectures on various types of mental illness and were given the full tour of the hospital so that I saw parts I had not visited before, including the male end of the wards and the sick bay. What impressed me about the male wards was the lack of smell; somehow they seemed to cope better with the endless 'accidents' which were forever having to be cleaned up on the female wards. The sick bay was for the care of those patients, who, in the course of time, would succumb to physical as well as mental illnesses. The ward that upset me most was the one where Down's syndrome adults were housed. As children these people had been hidden away as shameful and had grown old in these grim surroundings.

Later I was sent to nurse in the sick bay which I found more rewarding. One old lady was brought in suffering from pneumonia; poor soul, she probably hadn't had a clear thought in her head for many a long year. Her name was Jane, she was painfully thin and because of her condition she was as stiff as a board. We were instructed to get her up into a chair every day, but were hard put to settle her into it as she was unable to bend. She was given a whole barrage of antibiotics but, try as we might, she suffered from terrible bed sores on the back of her thin body, so that it was possible to see the bones of her spine when we carefully dressed her sores. The pneumonia gradually subsided and we continued to care for her, but when it came again they gave her more antibiotics. Poor soul, I felt that it would have been a kindness to let the infection give her a peaceful death, instead of having to suffer as she did.

Many things upset me about that place. One was that each patient had a personal allowance which was the balance left from their pensions after the money for their care had been deducted. The Ward Sisters administered this money and there was a shop on the premises that sold sweets and chocolates. The Sisters would purchase these on the patients' behalf and store everything in a large room next to the office. Occasionally they might bring out a tin of sweets to pass around the patients, but more often than not the goods went out in the Sisters' bags. Everyone knew what went on, but no one dared to speak out.

Meanwhile Auntie Ethel was admitted to the RVI for a

gall-bladder operation, so I fitted in my job, the care of the children, running the house and visiting her at every opportunity. Fortunately she recovered well and was sent to a convalescent hospital out near Consett where she was well looked after until she was fit enough to come home.

It was important to find some sort of a career structure for Anne and Paul. Anne's office job didn't last long but at the age of 17 we discovered that she could become a cadet-nurse at the RVI prior to commencing general nursing training, if she felt that that was what she would like to do. Her application was successful and she went as a live-in cadet, which eased the accommodation situation somewhat. One of the Officers at the Salvation Army arranged through one of his contacts for Paul to start work at the office of a quantity surveyor where he would also have the opportunity to learn the job and take his exams.

Louie had taken to visiting on a regular basis, and when Auntie Ethel was at the convalescent home he took Auntie Maryon and me out to visit her in his car. We had become close, and when he suggested that the children and I should move into his house, it seemed the ideal solution to our problems. He owned a large three-bedroomed Edwardian terraced house not far from Woodburn and nearer to school for Cathleen and Christopher. So we moved out of Woodburn, probably to Auntie Ethel's relief. Things went quite well to start with. I continued to work at St Nicholas' while Louie was a civil servant working from one of the local offices. His job was to fill in when anyone was off sick for any length of time, and to interview people over a far-flung area. Often he was away all week doing visits in Cumbria on the other side of the country. As an arrangement it went well for us both, although I knew it was nothing like the close and trusting commitment I had had with Ron.

While realising that Auntie Ethel was glad to have her

own place to herself once more, I would be forever grateful to her for giving us all a home when we so desperately needed it. Soon however, I began to find it harder to cope with a large house as well as the family, especially as I often had to work over weekends and was unable to spend time with them. Also things were changing at the hospital. A house on the premises had been set up to take four or five ladies at a time, and the less infirm among the patients were settled in there with a nurse. They were taken out and about, taught how to shop and to cook and generally look after themselves, prior to being discharged into council flats to fend for themselves. It was the beginning of 'Care in the Community'. Within a few years the whole structure of that huge hospital would be altered and, in the course of time, the very valuable land sold for building executive housing. Although I did not know or even guess this at the time, I knew I could no longer carry on with the long hours and the heavy work.

On my next day off I went to the Employment Exchange in town for an interview. Apart from passing my School Leaving Certificate I had very few qualifications that would suit me for not only a job, but one with a career structure. Had I been able to do typing and shorthand no doubt I would have been offered an office job, but I made it quite clear that I was the sole support of my four children and that a dead-end job was not acceptable. They therefore suggested that I apply to the DHSS, the Department of Health and Social Security as it was then known, whose central office was based in Newcastle and to which I had applied when I was enquiring about starting to pay National Insurance while I was still in South Africa. The unexpected outcome had been the award of a widow's pension at a reduced rate, and for that I was most grateful. They gave me the application forms to take away and once more I asked Archie Morrison and Ruby Collingwood-Stewart to be my referees. I waited anxiously for a reply.

Anne had not settled at the hospital and the Army arranged for her to go and work in one of their Children's Homes in London. I was not happy with her decision and I went along to the local police station to ask them if I could prevent her from going. After asking me how old she was and where she would be working, they said there was no way I could object even though at that time 21, not 18, was the age when parental responsibility fell away. And so all the arrangements were made for her and she went to live in a place of which I knew only the address.

Eventually I was called for an interview at DHSS Central Office, taking with me my School Leaving Certificate. I was warned not to leave my current job as it was uncertain when I was likely to be called. However, after an awful bout of flu I felt so worn out that just after Christmas 1968 I resigned from the hospital. The Matron asked to see me to try and persuade me to stay and very kindly said that 'we need nurses of your calibre,' but my mind was made up. Luckily, on the January 10th 1969 I received a letter from the DHSS informing me that I had been accepted into the department as a clerical assistant and assigned to the Central Office. I was to report at 8.15 am on January 20th to room 139N at Longbenton.

The last paragraph of the letter spelt out some extremely high-minded sentiments:

I should like to take this opportunity of extending to you a warm welcome on joining the Department. The Service of which you are about to become a member has high standards and a fine tradition and you will, I am sure, get much satisfaction from the opportunities this Department will give you of helping your fellow citizens and of pursuing a happy and successful career.

So, almost exactly a year after arriving back in England, I set out on my ultimate career.

2

Newcastle sits on the north bank of the swiftly flowing Tyne and was a well-established community long before many of the Midland cities that the Industrial Revolution spawned. The Romans had appreciated the military value of the site and had built a bridge at the first navigable part of the river before swinging their frontier defence system, Hadrian's Wall, from Wallsend across the hills to the West coast in AD 122. Before that, Christianity had been established at Melrose Abbey and Lindesfarne Priory by St Cuthbert, whose remains were buried at Durham even before that great cathedral sprang up, while the very name 'Newcastle' came from the fortifications built in 1080 by Robert, the son of William the Conqueror.

The city itself had a long history of heavy industry such as armaments, shipbuilding and steam turbines, all on the back of the shipment of coal from the Durham and Northumberland coal mines. The town centre consisted of many fine buildings constructed in the early 1800s by architect John Dobson and could equal any found in Regent Street in London, but its industrial decline between the wars had brought much unemployment.

At the point where Newcastle stood on the north and Gateshead on the south, the steep sides of the Tyne Valley meant that some remarkable feats of engineering had been required to build bridges to span the river. The arrival of the railways resulted in the building of the High Level Bridge which took trains across the river on its upper level, and other traffic on the roadway below. Some twenty years later the Swing Bridge was built at the river level, well named as it could be swung wide to let water traffic through. Two others, the Redheugh and the Scotswood bridges were added until, in pride of place, the Tyne Bridge was built. I was told, although I have no idea if this is true, that it was the precursor of the Sydney Harbour Bridge, and certainly at a quick glance one might be mistaken for the other.

Many of the city streets were named after the men who designed and built the centre of town, such as Clayton and Grainger Street and Eldon Square, while Pilgrim, Nun and Blackfriars Street harked back to the city's medieval beginnings. Several well-established department stores such as Fenwicks, Binns and Bainbridges catered for the many shoppers flooding in from far and near, and one of the largest branches of Marks and Spencer was a magnet for Norwegians sailing into the Tyne on pre-Christmas trips.

This was the city to which I had returned, and now it was time to take stock. A year on from our arrival I was satisfied with the job I now had and looked forward to furthering my career in the civil service. For the children there were pluses and minuses. I was not too happy with Anne's departure to London; it was a city I did not know and I felt that at 17 she was too young to be away from home. Brought up in South Africa, she was somewhat unsophisticated, the prevailing, and often only, interest on her horizon being *Top of the Pops*. She was convinced, as with so many teenagers, that she knew it all. Working in a Children's Home run by the Salvation Army seemed a reasonably safe pursuit until I had a letter telling me that she was now working as an au pair for a New Zealand couple who had a toddler and twin babies. The parents planned to return to New Zealand so the wife had gone back to work to help to earn the money for their fares. How long this job could last was therefore doubtful on more than one count. I couldn't imagine my young daughter coping for very long with three under-fives!

I contacted a friend, Brigadier Neeve, who had it seemed been instrumental in finding Anne the post at the Children's Home. She suggested that I should come to London and stay with her. She would then go with me to this new address where I could see for myself where Anne was and how she was coping. At the same time I made an appointment at the Salvation Army Headquarters asking for an interview.

Ethel Neeve met me at Kings Cross station and we went by bus to her little flat in north London. The next day we caught a bus that took us on a long tortuous journey to the southern suburbs of London and at last we found the house where Anne was working. She was most surprised to see us but I was pleased to see that the place was clean and well furnished, and when the young couple for whom she was working came home from work we found them to be most pleasant and very concerned for Anne's welfare. Other than that there was nothing more I could do, so we left and took the long bus journey back to Ethel's flat.

The next day she went with me to the Army Headquarters where I had a long interview with a sympathetic lady Officer. After hearing my story she agreed with me that there seemed very little point in hanging on to my commission. As Ethel said later that night over a cup of cocoa, it wasn't me who left the Army, it was the Army who left me, and truth to tell it was quite obvious that there was no place for me and my family in the UK set up.

So I returned to Newcastle, sent the Army my resignation, and at the same time had a cheque made out for the money they had sent me for my fare to the UK and returned it to them.

Paul settled in well to the surveyor's office and made friends with the other young trainees working there, while Christopher attended the local comprehensive which was not easy for him as it had been discovered in South Africa that he was dyslexic. But at the school he now attended they did not seem to be aware of such a thing, and he found it hard to keep up. After his first year there he would transfer to the senior school which was some distance away up Benton Road near the entrance to the Central Office where I was now working. At the nursery school a most dedicated teacher had spent much time with Cathleen, so that now she was talking quite well, but soon it would be time for her to start in the first-year reception class.

My first day at Central Office, known locally as 'The Ministry', began with a group of new starters attending an induction class. Here we had the pension system explained to us. My position seemed to be in some doubt, being a widow, but was soon resolved – I was on the same footing as the other women. It was explained that, to save a lot of bureaucracy, money was not deducted from our salaries as such, but when pay increases were awarded a reduced rate was given to take account of pension provisions. However, the married men therefore received a slightly lower pay rate than the women, as their pension also made provision for a wife or widow, while a woman's had none for a husband or widower.

We were then told where we would be working and provided with a map and an explanation of the layout of the offices. This was essential because, like Topsy, Central Office had 'just growed'. The initial buildings had been, I believe, a military hospital with long corridors and many 'spurs' leading off them. More recently, a large four- or five-storey building had risen to house the increasingly complex system. We were told that if we got lost we should not hesitate to ask for directions, and I had a vision of poor benighted souls wandering around forever lost like the Flying Dutchman.

I was to work in room 103, the post-opening room. This turned out to be an enormous room with groups of desks down both sides, while at the far end a huge space was left for large baskets on wheels to be filled from the many sacks of mail delivered throughout the course of the day. This was January, the windows were all tightly shut and it was hardly possible to see across the room for the thick smoke from countless cigarettes.

I had been taken on as a Clerical Assistant, or CA, the lowest clerical grade of all because, I was told, my School Leaving Certificate was not considered to be of the same high standard as the current O-level exams. However, it did ensure that I was given a permanent situation, rather than having to work on a temporary basis for anything up to a year.

The post room dealt with mail coming in from all around the country and also from overseas. Each section dealt with the mail for a particular part of the work done on the site: pensions, records, overseas pensions and family allowances, the latter being the section to which I was assigned. I was provided with a pen and a date stamp. The date stamp was issued from a locked cupboard and was listed in the record book, as it had on it a number which was personal to me. The mail was roughly sorted into the various sections at the end of the room, the envelopes slit open on a machine, then the family allowance mail was opened by our section, date stamped and sorted into groups according to the last two digits in the allowance number if there was one or, if not, alphabetically, ready to be sent down to the index department. The majority of the mail consisted of claim forms duly sent in using the stamped addressed envelope supplied, which helped to identify the letters as they arrived.

Valuables such as returned order books and postal orders for paying back overpayments were collected and collated by a CO or Clerical Officer, the next grade up. Two EOs or Executive Officers held sway, one on each side of the room, and should a birth or death certificate be damaged by the opening machine they would arrange for a copy to be obtained in its place.

The job was soon learned, and it was possible to have long conversations with the surrounding girls – most of the staff were women – to while away the time. There were rumours of some offices where those in charge insisted on complete silence during the course of the day, obviously a throwback to more Dickensian ways of administration, but we were not so penalised.

The girls were a good crowd. One had a brilliant son who had won a place at Oxford, but who, according to his mother, was barely able to tie his own shoelaces. She bemoaned this fact, often ending with the comment, 'but his father is only a milkman'. Poor soul, she had been taken on as a temporary office worker and at a later stage for some reason she was given a month's notice. There was nothing wrong with her work, but at that time it was possible to do things like that so I was doubly glad that I had been given permanent status.

Later on I was transferred to the section dealing with mail from all corners of the world, most of which was claiming retirement pensions. I realised that when I was still in South Africa, and had written to Central Office asking if I should start paying contributions as I was considering returning to England, my letter would have passed through this section. I remember how moved I was to receive what was, as I later realised, the standard letter saying how sorry they were to hear of my husband's death. It had felt like a hand of sympathy and friendship held out to me at that time.

This was brought to mind by an irate letter from a lady demanding to know why it was taking so long for her claim to be settled. 'After all,' she wrote, 'all you have to do is take an order book out of its slot and send it to me!' Little did she know how prolonged the investigations could be in tracking down insurance payments over the course of the years. Which was why it was so important for a claim form to be date stamped, as under the 'late claim' provisions, in certain circumstances payment could be made for the six months prior to a claim, as had happened in my case. The lump sum of one year's benefit had made a good nest egg to put in the building society to pay for my ultimate return to England with the children.

The date stamps proved invaluable on another occasion. Someone had sent in postal orders for some reason, but they had failed to arrive on the section dealing with the case. It was an easy task to find out who had dealt with the mail. Not only that, the thief had taken the orders to the Post Office on site and cashed them there. It transpired that she was a young girl who, finding herself pregnant and desperate for money, had succumbed to temptation. She left quietly and no action was taken against her.

Another case was quite weird, however. One of the few men working in the post room was a fellow who suffered from some sort of dwarfism. While not very much shorter than his contemporaries, he had a strangely dried-up complexion and often made barbed comments in my direction about 'married women who just worked for pin money'. As I did not tell all and sundry that I was a widow with four children I just ignored him, but then complaints came in that birth certificates had been returned to claimants with lewd comments scrawled on the back of them, and once more the culprit was soon found by using the date stamp system. Poor fellow, he was obviously very disturbed and he too quietly disappeared from our ranks.

One other mystery had intrigued the post opening section for some years. Every so often postal orders were sent in without any covering letter or explanation and it had proved impossible to discover from whom they had originated. Was it a guilty conscience? Or did someone think this was the way to pay for their National Insurance? The mystery was never solved while I was there, but all the payments were faithfully recorded and the money banked.

I now ran into another problem. I had taken, and passed

my driving test at the first try when I was 17. When we went to live in South Africa my licence, then renewable every year, had lapsed. For several years I cheerfully drove around without a current licence until, when I was to become a Salvation Army worker, I thought I had better make an honest woman of myself, and duly went down to the testing grounds, to take and pass my test once more.

Now back in England, I discovered that I could only drive using my South African licence for six months before taking a further test. So, using Louie's little Mini, I went off to take my third driving test, thinking to myself that it would be very ironic if I failed this one after driving for so many years. However, all was well. The Driving Inspector said he thought I had done quite well, as many of the expatriates he tested were used to driving in the middle of dirt roads miles from any other traffic, but I assured him that the Johannesburg traffic could knock spots off anything the Newcastle roads could throw up.

Louie had been in the Air Force during the war, and had been shot down and spent a long time in a prisoner-of-war camp until the end of the war. He now ran an Air Cadets group some 15 miles north of Newcastle and would set off once a month all dressed up in an Air Force Officer's uniform to conduct the various cadet activities. Christopher went once or twice but wasn't too keen and soon dropped it. Somewhat older than me, Louie struck quite an imposing figure, his remote Italian heritage having left him with a Mussolini-type nose set in a heavy face. Not what you could call good-looking, but naively I thought that I needn't worry about any undue competition from elsewhere on that account.

While he was off on these trips, I took up my regular visits to my maternal aunts, May and Elsie. Both were now widows, each with one son. Elsie's son Peter lived in Leeds with his wife and their three sons. May's son David lived in Brighton. His marriage to his Danish wife, Lisa, had recently broken up and she had returned home taking the two children with her. Elsie, the eldest aunt, still lived in her nice little rented flat on Biddlestone Road in Heaton, while May had moved into a bungalow just off the coast road shortly before her husband Alfie died in Walkergate Hospital. The nursing sister of the ward at that time was called Meg, and as Alfie's illness had been protracted, May and Meg had become very friendly. So when Meg needed a place to live, she moved in with May as a boarder.

The bungalow therefore became a centre of various activities involving May and Meg's friends, Elsie, me and anyone else who cared to come. Friday night was hairdressing night and we would wash and set each other's hair and share all the gossip. Some nights the Ouija board came out but that was mostly a non-starter, perhaps because no one troubled to push the glass round to make any sense.

The biggest success, however, was the crystal ball man. Of short stature and bundled up in many coats and scarves, a damp hanky ever at the ready, he would be seated in the kitchen while each lady took it in turns to pay up and have the crystal ball read. Often he could be amazingly accurate, as when he told a doctor's young wife that she was pregnant almost before she knew herself. At other times I noticed that he would have a favourite calamity about to happen. At one time it might be a broken leg, then next week it would be a sprained ankle. On one occasion a lady I worked with at 'The Ministry' came out looking puzzled as he hadn't been able to tell her anything. I was not surprised really, as she was the most negative character I had ever met and I had invited her hoping to put a bit of spice into her life! His favourite line was that 'the Norwegians' had been for a reading. Who or what they were I never found out, but as he left one night he said to Meg, 'I can sense death in this house.' Later she told May in confidence, but it came at a time when Elsie had confessed that she had a lump in her breast. It appeared she had had it for quite some time but had been too frightened to mention it to anyone. Persuaded at last to see her GP she was rushed into hospital for an immediate mastectomy followed by radiation treatment. But it must have been obvious that she had left it too late as no chemotherapy was ever suggested, and as her health deteriorated she moved into the bungalow with May, Meg doing sterling work helping to care for her.

Her son Peter, meanwhile, even as the cancer spread throughout Elsie's body, was conspicuous by his absence, and May would slip out at night to phone him from the local phone box and beg him to visit his mother, who was asking for him. By the time he came, it was too late. She died on a Friday and Louie and I raced to the Registrar with the doctor's note to obtain her death certificate before they closed for the weekend. Peter arrived the next day and was able to start the funeral proceedings straight away. It was a sombre service in the brand new Catholic Church on Heaton Road and later the burial in the local cemetery. None of us knew the Catholic liturgy apart from Louie, so the responses were muted. Poor Elsie, she lived for her son and her grandsons and never tired of knitting them all splendid pullovers, but her dearest wish to see Peter before she died was not granted.

The place where the Air Cadets met was also the scene of a social club which Louie liked to go to as well. Reluctantly I went along with him, as it wasn't really my scene. The air would be thick with cigarette smoke, and there would be some sort of entertainer, but if one was not available Louie would play the piano. He was a natural player, never needing music and able to pound out any requests. His greatest joy was to sing and play 'My Way' to rapturous applause, after which we would all settle down to a game of bingo. I was no drinker and, in fairness, nor was he. A couple of pints would see him through the night, but I began to notice that he would make a beeline for any female who gave him half a glance, and I found that very unsettling.

These were the days of the first cheap package holidays, so it was decided that we would go to Spain, taking Christopher and Cathleen, while Paul would stay at his friend's house. We booked for a fortnight in June at the grand price of £26 each.

Meanwhile, Auntie Ethel was far from well. The doctor, who so rarely examined her, was called in and said her heart was weak and she should have complete rest for a few weeks. We made enquiries and found a rest home on Osbourne Road called The White House. As nursing care was not needed it seemed like a good idea, as they had a nice big downstairs room available, a pleasant communal room and a good menu. With hindsight, I wished I had taken unpaid leave of absence from my job at Longbenton in order to care for her, but I had only recently started there and additionally I needed the money to pay my share of the expenses at Louie's house.

She moved in very happily and we visited her most evenings. Her sister-in-law Nancy with her second husband, as well as my cousin Bill, were all regular visitors, and we thought that before long the doctor would pronounce her well enough to go home. She got on well with the other ladies there and one of them insisted she should come and look at her room. Never able to refuse a request Ethel set off with her, not realising the lady was up on the third floor. She never really recovered from the climb up those stairs in her weakened state and we were called urgently one evening by Bill to come quickly. We found her in bed in a comatose state; she had been settled in her room by the staff who had thought her electric fire was turned on. It transpired that only the decorative light was showing, but there was no heat coming from the bars. Chilled through, and weakened by her climb up the stairs, this was how Nancy, George and Bill had found her that evening. We had collected her sister

Maryon on our way there, and as we gathered around her bed I held her hands as her breathing slowed and eventually stopped. It was March 5th 1969.

The funeral was held at the crematorium and one or two representatives from the WVS came to pay their respects, but she had been a quiet lady and otherwise only the immediate family members were there. The lady next door to Woodburn had offered to do a 'tea' for us so we all went back there afterwards. Later Maryon cornered me and asked me if I knew that Ethel had intended to leave Woodburn to me. I recalled that while I was still in South Africa shortly after Ron died that she had written to me to say that this was what she intended to do, but I did not know if she actually had. Maryon seemed to think that she had, but what she wanted to know was whether I would let her have it as she wanted to leave St Mary's Mount where she was currently living. This did not unduly surprise me, as the place had been sadly neglected in the years that she had owned it. Never a great housekeeper, she would use a room until it was no longer habitable and then move on to the next one. She currently had a caravan in the drive from where she was supposed to conduct her dog-breeding business, but it was anyone's guess whether any of the rooms were in a fit state to live in, as she never encouraged visitors. Meanwhile I knew that the council were making noises about a compulsory purchase of the property and there was some dispute about the meagre price they were prepared to pay. Her solicitor said she could take it to the High Court in London but it might be an expensive business, so at present it was all on hold.

I said I couldn't really say at that time, in fact even as we spoke I was still trembling from the shock of Ethel's death, but at the back of my mind was the thought that, if the house had been left to me, I could leave Louie and be more independent. There were things about him that I was unhappy about, his attitude to the children for one thing. It was as though he was a sergeant-major viewing his troops when he came in last to sit with us at dinner. He was very abrupt with Cathleen and would glare at Christopher if he joined us in the lounge in the evening. I felt we deserved better, but I had nowhere else to go at that point.

Time passed. Bill was one of the executors of Ethel's will and one day at work I was called to the telephone. It was Bill and he had bad news for me. Apparently Maryon and Ethel had gone together to make their wills and the result had been that they had left everything to each other in the first place, and the gift of Woodburn to me had been added on afterwards. As Ethel had died first, the house and everything else all went to Maryon. I returned to my desk in shock, hardly able to believe how Ethel's wishes had turned out, but there was nothing I could do.

The time came round for the holiday we had booked. With airports on practically every doorstep nowadays, it is hard to believe how difficult it was to get to our destination. With economy in mind, we took the bus from Newcastle to London. It seemed endless. We had gone overnight and were able to sleep a little on the way. Arriving at Victoria, we spent the day in London visiting the National Gallery, Parliament Square, and finally queuing for the visitors' gallery at the House of Commons in the afternoon. Little did I realise that in years to come I would be intimately involved with the goings-on in that great building.

In the early evening we made our way back to Victoria bus station where we picked up our scheduled bus out to Gatwick Airport. The journey seemed never-ending and it was after dark by the time we reached the airport. We shuffled to the check-in desk and after what seemed a long wait we finally boarded our plane and set off. Our destination was

Genova Airport and dawn was just breaking as we arrived and were herded onto the waiting buses. There followed another interminable drive until we reached the coast and the bus began to stop at one hotel after another, dropping passengers off as we went along. Ours seemed to be the last one, but as we smelled the warm air and looked around at the quiet square before entering the hotel, I felt it boded well for our holiday.

We tumbled gratefully into bed to catch up on some lost sleep, but we soon discovered that the air of peace and tranquillity of our arrival only lasted for a few short hours in the early morning. The streets all went from east to west or north to south and there were no traffic lights at each crossroads. Traffic included buzzing motor scooters as well as small cars, and all were equipped with loud horns. We awoke to a cacophony of sound which was to accompany us all through our holiday.

The town of Callella was very pleasant though, and we enjoyed strolling through its narrow streets, visiting the many shops selling goods for the tourists and spending time on the beach. Chris and Cathleen loved it and I bought Chris some goggles and flippers and he played happily in the sea. Cathleen enjoyed digging holes and making sand castles and Louie sunbathed, while I tried to keep out of the sun as much as possible as I burned easily. The beach had what looked like sand, but when walked upon it turned out to be a fine grit which, combined with the heat, would strip the soles off the feet unless they were protected.

We spent one day going on the little local train to Barcelona where I enjoyed the pleasant city with its broad boulevards and its quirky cathedral, still in the process of being built after so many years, so we were told.

Our holiday was half-board and breakfasts could be taken as and when we wished. The evening meals were taken in two sittings with each guest having a regular place to sit.

We sat at a table with two middle-aged ladies, and one explained to us that she and her husband ran a pub in the Midlands so it was impossible for them to go on holidays together. So she went off several times a year with her friend and her husband took golfing trips from time to time. They were both very nice, but somehow I felt shy because of the fact that Louie and I were not married, added to which he began his usual act of paying more attention to these ladies than he did to me and the children. This was beginning to make me feel more and more uneasy and undermined my confidence, but there was little I could complain about.

Our two weeks came to an end and once more we faced the return journey by bus, by plane, by bus then again by bus, from London to Newcastle. As we travelled on the last lap, I also realised I had caught a cold and sat with a streaming nose and aching head.

3

The Central Office at Newcastle had a very active social club with various amusements such as dances and sporting activities. On their noticeboard I saw that there was a rifle club situated in the basement of the only multi-storey building on the site. So I went along and joined up. At the next session I told Louie where I was going and went along and had a lovely evening. I was no expert but in my teens, when we would regularly go to Spanish City at Whitley Bay, I always enjoyed the shooting galleries and generally found that I had quite a good aim. When I got back home I told Louie how much I had enjoyed it. He looked a bit thoughtful and then announced that as he was also a civil servant, he would be eligible to join the social club and next time he would come along with me. I was not entirely happy with this but there was nothing I could do, so at the next session we both went along.

I should have known it would not work out. As soon as we arrived it seemed that he singled out the only unattached female there and before long was exercising his charm on her, much to her delight. She then proceeded to patronise me, asking me whether or not I was paid weekly or monthly. With hindsight I should have told her to mind her own business, but I have always had a knee-jerk reaction to questions and usually find I have given an answer before weighing up what the question was all about. And so, my reply was 'Weekly,' to which I got a sneering reply, 'Oh, *I* get paid monthly.'

To many people this would not seem to be of any great

import – except that lowly CAs such as me were paid weekly, while upmarket COs got their pay monthly. That set the tone for the rest of the evening and I was effectively sidelined while the two conspirators had a whale of a time. That was my last visit to the rifle club and I started to wonder if this was a deliberate ploy on Louie's part to prevent me from undertaking any lone activities.

I had a letter from Anne which shook me up somewhat. She said that she was very unhappy in England, and she had gone to South Africa House in London. They had told her that they would 'repatriate' her to South Africa but because she was under 21 she would need my written permission. It seemed a bit odd to me as Anne had been born in England and had a British passport but I had no way of knowing what the facts of the matter were. However a decision was required.

What a dilemma to be in! If I agreed to her going, I knew that she had friends and relations in Johannesburg and that in all probability she would be well cared for, but would I ever see her again? On the other hand if I refused, her resentment might be such that we would lose touch in any event. After a great deal of thought I decided that I had very little choice but to agree to her going, if that was what she wished to do, so I wrote and gave her my consent.

At work, although I was friendly with all the women, my greatest friend turned out to be Joe, the CO who was in charge of the valuables. Joe lived with his wife and two daughters in a flat on the other side of Chillingham Road and had been a civil servant since leaving the forces. He was a small man but with a load of kindness, and we hit it off and enjoyed our conversations so much that we would go for a stroll every lunchtime and put the world to rights. Our working hours were set in stone, 8 am to 4.30 pm with an hour for lunch, so that by 12.30 sandwiches were soon eaten and it was good to get out of the stuffy atmosphere of Room 103. I have always found it easier to get onto a good wavelength with men, rather than women, without there being any misunderstandings about motive, perhaps because my father had been a great influence on me in the absence of a mother. Whatever the reason, I looked forward to our chats although I never shared with Joe my misgivings over Louie.

The 'Flower Power' and Carnaby Street influence of the 1960s seemed to have largely by-passed the north-east without leaving any undue effect. While living in South Africa we had read of the Profumo affair with a certain degree of astonishment, and during the invasion of Egypt over the Suez Canal we had been firmly on the British side and could hardly believe the climbdown that ensued after America et al. withdrew their support and insisted that Britain withdraw. So now I had returned to a country that seemed to have lost its bearings as well as its empire and was swinging in the wind as it looked for its part to play in the modern world. Our once proud country, which had fought so valiantly for its freedom, seemed to have lost all credibility and standing in the world, added to which France refused to allow us any entry into the European Community. This seemed a very harsh blow considering how this country had given De Gaul sanctuary and support during the war. So our discussions were many and far ranging.

It was Joe who pointed out to me that promotion could be hastened by sitting the Civil Service exams, held annually. In addition there were night classes available to coach those aspiring to give it a go. I made some enquiries and in September enrolled for the next session of classes. These were held in an old-fashioned college in the centre of town and on the first evening, after everyone had registered, there were so many people that there were not enough desks for them all. However, classes took place on two nights a week, one for English and General Studies, and the other for Maths, and within a very short space of time we were whittled down to about twenty regulars. As winter came nearer it became necessary to wrap up warm with extra socks and fur-lined boots, as the janitor would turn the heating off once the day students had gone home and we could feel the warmth seeping away as we tried to concentrate on our studies.

I became friendly with a girl called Audrey who offered me a lift home in her car one night. I was most grateful as the wait for buses in the cold streets, after being chilled to the bone in the college, was anything but a pleasing prospect. It appeared that she lived a few miles further on from me, but she said she would be happy to pick me up as well, if I would like. I was delighted and told Louie of my good fortune. He had not been available to give me any lifts as the classes clashed with his Air Cadet activities, so when the time came for the next class, Louie, all togged up in his Air Force Officer's uniform, insisted on walking with me down to the end of the street where Audrey had arranged to meet me. I had no choice but to introduce him to Audrey and as I held open the car door he leant in, turning on all the charm he could muster before I was finally able to seat myself. I sat fuming next to a bemused Audrey, who was probably wondering what all that was about.

By now I had alarm bells ringing right, left and centre, and I thought back to when I was a young teenager recovering from a bout of jaundice as it was known then (no doubt it was hepatitis). I had been sent to stay with Louie and his wife who were living in a house in Redcar after his discharge from the Air Force. At that time they had two small toddlers and Mary was extremely well organised and did not seem to need any help I might have been able to give. I had thought it a bit odd that Louie would knock on my bedroom door every morning and bring me in a cup of tea. Even odder was that he offered to take me to the speedway where the Pepper Brothers were making a name for themselves. Mary stayed at home of course, but on the way back he had walked along with his arm around my waist. Perhaps such attention explained Mary's rather cool attitude, but at that age I was not up to sorting out what went on in adult relationships. I wondered if Mary had been treated to the same sort of situation that I now found to be occurring more and more often.

Louie's trips to the Air Cadets seemed to result in his returning home at a later and later hour, the explanation being that the attached social club could keep the bar open for as long as they liked and they would be joined by the late-night bus drivers as they came off shift. This kind of thing probably also accounted for the manner in which Mary had finally left him. After having a large family she had gone back to teaching and had obviously saved the money she earned. When she had sufficient she bought and furnished a house in the next street, all unknown to Louie. One day when he came home from work, he was confronted by this determined lady telling him that she was leaving and taking the children with her. There was nothing he could do and, as Catholics, there was no question of a divorce. To me this smacked of a woman who had suffered years of humiliation but who, having decided that enough was enough, had laid her long-term plans accordingly.

It must have been a short time after she left that I returned to England, because I remember Auntie Ethel telling me that Louie was living on his own just up the street. Not long after, she said she had bumped into him at the shops and told him that I was living with her, and then, bingo ... at our front door was Louie in his officer's uniform, to a huge welcome from the aunts who remembered him as a little boy. It all began to make sense. I was the next needy lady and I had fallen for it, hook, line and sinker. The words frying pan and fire came to mind. In fact I seemed to have leapt through a succession of both frying pans and fires, but what could I do? Realistically, at this moment, not a lot.

Having experienced the feelings of helplessness during our years in South Africa when Ron had succumbed to alcoholism I was well versed in keeping my financial independence, and although Louie and I lived together I paid my share of the bills and took care of the children's needs from my own earnings. But the house was his and I had nowhere else to go. I would just have to sit things out and put as good a face on things as I could. I could not believe that I had landed myself and my children in this situation.

Ron and I had had our problems, especially when he had become an alcoholic and I had had to take on the responsibility of keeping our family afloat financially, but throughout it all, I had known that he had a deep love for me, and while for a long time I had lost much of my respect for him, still he was the one for me. We had spent five wonderful years working together after he had stopped drinking, and he was my soulmate. When he died so suddenly it was as if I had been torn in two, so blended were our personalities. So while I had not expected to find another such deep relationship, I had never expected to be so emotionally sidelined by the person who was supposed to be my partner. I felt not only unloved, but also undervalued, and I was not prepared to put up with it.

Christmas was approaching and I had a letter from Anne. The possible return to South Africa was not mentioned, as she had left her au pair job and was working as a receptionist in a small business. She told me she had met a lovely young man called Dave. He had long hair, she said, and he played in a group, no doubt the reason for her deciding to stay in England. I could not have been more thankful, however long his hair was! She asked if she could come to Newcastle to spend Christmas with us but the idea terrified me. I could just imagine Louie in his element, dancing rings around my daughter while I had no choice but to stand and watch. I did not even trust him to keep his hands off her, so with a heavy heart I wrote to Anne and suggested that it would be a good idea to stay down there and get to know Dave's family.

I had spent the previous New Year's Eve on my own, as Louie had explained that he always went to stay with his elder brother in Middlesbrough. This year, however, I was to accompany him and the boys would stay at home with Cathleen. I was not all that eager to go as I had met his brother, and while he seemed a nice enough fellow who had been a widower for some years, he really wasn't my cup of tea. However, Louie seemed keen that I should, so we drove down on New Year's Eve and went to his brother's house where we were to spend the night after the party we were to attend.

It was held in a huge social club and when we found our table it was already occupied by a crowd who had obviously spent much time together before. Among them was one large, overblown, middle-aged lady who welcomed Louie with open arms. He was, it seemed, her long-lost pal. Her husband looked on morosely. We sat down, and this time I was determined not to be a sidelined onlooker. I began to make myself pleasant to the husband who was soon responding with enthusiasm; no doubt he too was fed up with playing second fiddle to whoever she decided to attach herself to. It was not long before she realised what I was up to and, with a proprietary glare, she engaged her husband's attention once more and dropped Louie like a hot brick. That was her taken care of.

Among the group was an unattached fellow whose regular girlfriend had been unable to come to the party and before long, seeing the murderous looks I was getting from Louie, he asked me to dance. We had great fun on the floor, laughing and joking for the rest of the night, and after the party was over he took me back to Louie's brother's house in his car, with I have to admit quite a lot of what we used to call 'necking' going on before I got out.

The next morning you could have cut the atmosphere with a knife. I knew I had behaved badly, but Louie was a man who deserved all he got. We set off back to Newcastle but when we got to Darlington he parked the car in the centre of town, got out and walked off. I sat and waited for a while, then wondering where he had got to, I also got out and went to look around the corner to see if I could see him. He must have been watching for me to do just that, because when I returned to where the car had been parked, it was gone and I was stranded. It was New Year's Day with no one about and no transport, so I didn't know what to do.

Eventually I found a phone box, looked up his brother's phone number and rang him to ask him to come and get me. Thankfully he did and took me back to his house where his girlfriend was still staying. They made me a meal and I rang Auntie May and told her what had happened. She suggested I send the children round to her, so I rang them and told them to go straight round to her, as I didn't know what Louie might do. His brother said he had probably gone to cry on the shoulder of an old girlfriend of his, who had been in the background all through the marriage to Mary.

After I was rested, Louie's brother drove me back to Newcastle and offered to come into the house with me, but I declined with many grateful thanks for his help. This was a situation I would deal with myself. Louie was in the kitchen, and during the ensuing conversation I made him see that I would never have flirted with anyone else if it hadn't been for his behaviour. I hinted that perhaps we could set our relationship on a different footing and each live independently, and he seemed to find the idea of this intriguing, but I knew in my heart that I would never trust him again and that I had to find a way out. He was wondering where the children were, as I am sure he felt that because of them I was a captive housekeeper, but I didn't tell him, I merely said I was going out to think things over. I put on a heavy coat and left the house.

It was only a short walk to Jesmond Dene, deserted on this cold New Year's Day. What a start to 1970. Soon I would be 40 and my situation seemed to be more desperate than ever. With tears streaming down my face I walked the well-known paths, my hands thrust deep into my pockets. If only Woodburn had been left to me I would have had a safe haven for myself and the children. If only Louie had been a different sort of person.

I had realised quite early on in my widowhood that I would not want to live alone for the rest of my life. After all, I had only been 35. I also knew that the chances of finding anyone in my own age group who was free, and even if free, who would want to take on someone with four children, were very remote indeed. So the meeting with Louie had seemed a miracle. He had a large house, he was on his own, he was someone I had known off and on for most of my life. The family liked him and I thought he would provide a stable background for the children to grow up in. Who would have taken him to be the manipulating philanderer I had uncovered!

As the short winter day began to fade, I dried my tears and made my way to Woodburn, hoping to find Auntie Maryon there. It wasn't likely that she would be out, with all the shops being shut, and sure enough I found her at home. I told her that I would have to leave Louie, without going into all the details, and she didn't seem unduly surprised. She asked me what I would do, and I said that perhaps I could find a furnished flat to rent. She knocked that idea on the head immediately because, as she said, landlords would not let a place to a woman on her own with so many children. I could see that she was right.

I knew that she had a friend who owned a house which had stood empty for some years overlooking the cricket

46

ground in Heaton, so after a long silence I tentatively asked her if she thought Miss C. might let me rent it. Her immediate response was to say no, she was quite sure that not only would she not let it, but additionally she would not even ask her. After more silence she said, 'Why don't you buy somewhere to live?'

'Well mainly,' I said, 'because I can't afford to.'

Another long period of thought, and then she said that if she were to lend me the deposit, would I be able, with my earnings, to afford the upkeep of a small flat? I gasped. The idea had never occurred to me, but providing I could get a mortgage, I was sure that I could manage, in fact I would make sure I would. I realised that she must have felt badly about inheriting Woodburn when she knew that Ethel had really intended it to go to me, and perhaps this was her way of helping me.

Feeling more optimistic than I had for some time, I thanked her for her offer and said I would be only too grateful to take her up on it. Then I left to go and retrieve the children from May's bungalow and returned to Louie. After they were all safely in bed that night I told Louie of Maryon's offer. Knowing that my aunt was to be involved, he gave in with good grace and said he would help me in my search for a flat for me and the children. That night I had the soundest sleep I had enjoyed for many months. At last there seemed to be some light on the horizon.

4

First of all I needed to find out if I would be able to get a mortgage, so I went once more to see my father's friend Archie Morrison, who was the manager of the Newcastle Building Society, the one at which Great-aunt Allie had deposited money for her nephews and nieces. I had known Archie and his wife when I was growing up and had often been a visitor at their house. His wife was profoundly deaf, poor soul, and their only son had gone to live and work in America as part of the current 'brain drain'. He welcomed me into his office and I told him of my plans, although I didn't enlarge upon my difficulties with Louie as I doubted that he would be aware of exactly where I had been living for the past two years or so. I outlined my income and my career prospects now that I was planning to work towards a promotion, and he was most sympathetic.

I told him about losing out to Maryon over Woodburn, but he seemed to think this was no bad thing as he felt I would have been unable to afford to run it. He obviously had no idea that Ethel had run it on a very limited income, but as I had often found in the past, many people were under the impression that our family were richer than they actually were. This was all to the good and I expect he also felt that, if I ran into trouble, Maryon would help me out, although personally I had absolutely no intention of ever finding myself in that situation. We discussed what repayments I might be able to afford and on that basis Archie gave me a rough idea as to what I could borrow and how much deposit would be needed.

So once the holidays were over I visited the local estate agent on Chillingham Road as I wanted to stay in the same area. The cheapest housing was to be found off the main road among the rows of terraced flats which had been built towards the end of the nineteenth century. Newcastle was probably unique in the design of these flats, as the upstairs with four main living rooms and the downstairs with three were always sold as a job lot, so that the buyer had occupation of either the upper or lower flat, which would come with a sitting tenant in the occupied one. Most of the tenancies were long term with very low protected rents. A tiny front garden would contain a path to both front doors, and at the back would be a yard with an open stairway for the upstairs flat, leading down to the outside toilet and a coal shed. Nothing fancy here, but such a pair of flats would provide a solid roof over our heads.

I would have preferred occupancy of an upper flat, giving an extra room, but a downstairs one would do as the rooms were all of a good size. Louie went with me and the first one we looked at was with vacancy of the upper flat, but I was concerned by the fact that it was the end one in the row. The wall surrounding the yard looked at imminent risk of falling down and would need very expensive pointing to make it safe.

There weren't many flats on the market at that time and I was beginning to get a bit desperate when we went to look at one on Chillingham Road itself, but down at the far end towards the railway line to the coast. This was really further out than I wanted to be, but the flat itself was a ground-floor one and had had the bathroom modernised, the back boiler taken out and an immersion heater and hot water cylinder installed. The young couple selling it were relocating to Wallsend from where they had originally come. It was in good decorative order with a wide passage off which was a large front room with bay window. At the back at the end of the passage was another smaller bedroom while the door to the right led into a good-sized living room. At the far side was a door and three steps leading down into the kitchen, fitted out with sink, draining board, and cupboards on both sides. Beyond it was the door into the small bathroom where a bath and hand basin had been squeezed in. The door to the yard led off from the kitchen and at the far end of the yard was the toilet, which had been nicely painted out, and the coal house. Heating was from the coal fire in the lounge and I would have to buy an electric oven as the gas supply had been taken out of the flat. Upstairs an elderly widow called Mrs Robson lived at a rent of a few shillings a week which was collected by an agent. All this was on the market for £1,800.

I went back to Maryon and asked her if she would like to come and look at the flat before I went any further, but she said she was happy to leave it up to me. I said that Archie Morrison had estimated that the deposit would be about £100, and she said I should go ahead and let her know when I wanted a cheque. I had managed to save a small amount so I would be able to pay the solicitor myself, but there was no money for anything like a survey. I would have to save hard during the time before completion to put money to one side for a few furnishings.

Meanwhile relations with Louie were tense, but he was still quite intrigued by my hint of some sort of a new relationship between us. I have no idea what he thought I had in mind, perhaps some sort of kinky swapping of partners, who knows. I remained mysterious, while intending to put as much space between us as possible once I had made the move to our new home.

Maryon came up trumps again. As well as Woodburn, she had also inherited its contents which were more than she needed, so she was able to let me have two beds, one double and one three-quarter size, as well as a dining table which had once belonged to Great-aunt Allie and the sideboard which had been my mother's. Meanwhile May and Meg had discovered the joy of duvets, and so I inherited the blankets and quite a lot of bed linen, some of which had been Auntie Elsie's. While still in South Africa I had bought an English women's magazine which was advertising a tea and dinner service that I quite liked, so with my return to the UK in mind, I had sent the money for it and had had it delivered to Auntie Ethel. Pots and pans were soon found in charity shops and a carpet shop on Shields Road sold offcuts which could be used at strategic points.

At last the day to move in came, and I experienced a tremendous feeling of relief as I sat in my own home in front of my own fire and in my own chair. I vowed that never again would I be dependent on someone else's whim or charity. This was the first place I could really call my own (and the building society's of course) and the sense of possession was overwhelming.

Louie hadn't completely given up, however, and suggested that in return for an occasional evening meal at my flat he would take me to the local supermarket to do my weekly shopping. This worked for a while but it soon dawned on him that his presence was not required so he announced that he would no longer be able to take me to the shops. This was all right by me, and we saw no more of him.

Supermarkets were just coming into their own, and Safeways had opened one down the road in Wallsend. It was some distance away, but I bought myself a shopping trolley and I would walk up to the top of Chillingham Road and catch the bus that would take me to Wallsend. There I would buy as much as I could stuff into the trolley then struggle to lift it back onto the bus for the trip home. One day I had overestimated what I could carry and got off the bus slung about with various bags and parcels, as well as the trolley. I just knew I wouldn't be able to stagger down the road with it all. Just then two young boys came along, so I called them over and asked them if they would like to earn a shilling each and help me home with the parcels. Bless them, they did. After that I made sure I took Chris or Paul with me.

The boys were great. Paul gave me £3 a week for his board and Chris took a newspaper round and contributed £1. I earned £10 a week and had £6 in widowed mother's allowance, and out of that I had to pay £16 a month mortgage repayments as well as the rates and electricity. I didn't have a washing machine so lugged the washing up to the launderette every week. The first one home, usually Christopher, lit the fire during the cold months, and the deal was that I cooked our meal and the boys washed up afterwards. At the weekend it was their responsibility to clean their own bedroom while I did the rest of the flat. Each fresh purchase we managed to make towards the greater comfort of our little home was celebrated as a great achievement.

We did not have a TV, which resulted in their friends all coming to our house, as in their own homes they had to keep quiet while their parents watched the telly. At our place we played cards and board games and it cost me a fortune in instant coffee. But I wouldn't have had it any other way as it meant I knew where my boys were and who their friends were.

At that time it was generally thought that it was not possible for women to get a mortgage. It was not something that had occurred to me and I had had no qualms about applying for one myself. However Meg, my Aunt May's boarder and friend, decided that if I could do it, so could she. She was well established in her profession as a nurse so soon found a flat for sale in a secluded part of Jesmond Vale and before long had moved in. To begin with she found it very difficult financially as she coped with all the extra money that had to be found for solicitors, rates and other expenses. If she hadn't been able to have meals with my aunt, she would have found it very hard going indeed.

I continued with my night classes. Cathleen always went to bed by seven o'clock, and the noise of the boys' friends never disturbed her, so I could go twice a week for my classes leaving her safely at home. The exams came and went, and while I waited for the results I thought it would be a good idea to go and see how Anne was doing. Most of my annual leave had to be kept for days off when any of the children were sick or needed to go to the doctor's, but I managed to earmark a week in June and wrote and invited myself to Anne's. Cathleen and I caught the London bus to Victoria bus station and then the train to East Croydon where Anne met us. She was living in a bedsit in Norbury and had a job as a receptionist somewhere.

We managed to squeeze in with her and I finally met Dave, he of the long hair. As all the young men wore their hair long at that time, my sons included, this was not out of the way, and it seemed that the group he had played with had died a death. Anne coyly showed me her packet of birth control pills, which was a bit of a relief. One of my worries had been that she might arrive back in Newcastle pregnant and alone, and I had already put my mind at rest by telling myself that if that happened, we would manage somehow. But thank goodness it was not to be.

I thought Dave was quite nice although not the man I had really envisaged for my daughter. He tended to put on a 'barrow boy' mien and seemed to be under the impression that anyone who came from the north-east was not dissimilar to a resident of Outer Mongolia. That apart, I thought he could be quite good for her as I realised she needed the stability of a good relationship. Cathleen and I enjoyed our week and I set off back to Newcastle on the bus with my mind at rest for Anne.

Soon my exam results arrived and I was pleasantly surprised

53

to find that out of the possible 300 marks I had only dropped about 30. The night classes had obviously paid off, as my maths had been very rusty after so many years. The next step was to be called for an interview which I have to say I found very enjoyable. I was asked how it was that I had made so many career changes over the years, which didn't take much explaining. They were also interested in the fact that I had lived in South Africa, as the anti-apartheid movement was at that time gathering momentum. I wasn't going to be drawn on that however, I merely said that the Africans were a very happy people. This was a time when protests of one sort or another were a feature of University life and the current one was against apartheid. Later of course, it would lose some support as the 'Ban the Bomb' campaign kicked in. There had recently been elections and for the first time in my life I had been able to vote in an election myself, due to a variety of circumstances. Voting had also been extended to 18-year-olds for the first time, and I told them that I had taken my eldest son along with me to vote. We discussed elections in general and I brought up the fact that in Australia voting was compulsory. I was asked what I thought of Dickens as a writer, so I told the truth and said I had never cared for him. Luckily for me, a recent biography had been reviewed in the papers, so I was able to say that by all accounts he was not a good husband or father himself. Even as I sat there the interviewers said among themselves that they thought I was very good material for promotion to CO '... or even further,' said one. I came out walking on air. A few weeks later I was notified that I had been promoted to Clerical Officer status and should report for duty at the Family Allowance section.

At that time, Family Allowances, as it was then called, was situated in a further series of army-type buildings some distance from the main Central Office complex, but initially we had to report to a room in the main building where the group of new recruits were gathered to be trained before starting on their new jobs. One of the instructors told us that he had been on the committee which had gathered to set the system up right at the beginning. He said that they had sat around and pondered over every eventuality that they could think of that might affect a family with children, but in his own words they found that they had only 'scraped the surface' of all the possible circumstances that could have a bearing on the claiming of Family Allowances.

The original concept was quite simple. For the first child in a family, no benefit was due. Once the second and subsequent children arrived, payment was made for each child. Post-war of course, it was in the country's interests to increase the population. The difficult bits, which were contained in thick books of instructions that were continually being amended, were called 'Change of circumstances'. Changes of address were among the simplest, lost order books were a minefield and the excuses were legion. Then there were circumstances when families broke up and children were shuttled from one parent to another; when they went into care; when they were in hospital; when their parents were 'itinerants' or 'travellers'; when they went or returned from abroad. These were some of the details that provided the bulk of the work.

I sat next to a lady called Agnes and we discovered that we lived fairly near to each other. So when our training session was over and we were allocated to our various sections, we would meet up in the early morning on Chillingham Road and walk, using shortcuts, to the offices This had a dual spin-off in that it was healthy and it was cheap. We had had a pay increase that year of about £1 a week, but at the same time the price of bread and bus fares had combined to pretty well wipe out any advantage.

Agnes was a bit older than me with two grown-up daughters, one at university and one married with young children. For many years her husband had worked as a manager at the

Co-operative Stores in Newcastle, then, to his dismay and distress, he was made redundant. He took it extremely badly as his job had been his whole existence, and before long, with no money coming in, Agnes did not know which way to turn as he refused to go and claim unemployment benefit. At last, in desperation, she went to the Employment Exchange herself and explained their predicament. They had been most sympathetic and promised her that an Inspector would visit their house without telling her husband what she had done, and explain to him that it was his right to claim from the benefit system into which he had paid all his life. And so it was done and he never suspected that Agnes had had a hand in it. Meanwhile she had seen an advert for a job at 'The Ministry', she applied and so we met. She was a good friend and we enjoyed our walks to work together each day.

The section I worked on was situated in a long room with windows on both sides and groups of desks along the left-hand wall. Sets of three desks were placed facing another set of three desks where the COs worked, while an EO held sway at his own desk just beyond. Behind each row of desks were shelves holding the ledgers containing the individual details of each family in the section of responsibility.

The Department were very good at helping with the transition from weekly to monthly pay, and paid me fortnightly for a while until I could move over to a monthly system, but money was still tight and every care had to be taken. It was amazing how many dishes could be made with mince as a base, and egg and chips were always a firm favourite with a can of baked beans to spice things up. That summer we would take picnics to the park up the road, and on a good day catch a bus down to the coast.

Paul took out a learner's licence and his friend from work let him learn to drive in his car. He passed his test and the two of them drove across France to Italy to watch the Formula One racing in Milan.

Louie, meanwhile, kept up his association with Auntie Maryon and would take her to the bingo at the Catholic Social Club on Heaton Road, so I knew when he moved yet another poor female into his home. This one was not only a bit younger, she was also pregnant. She had been one of the bus company staff who used to congregate at the Air Cadet Social Club after hours, so my instincts had not been far out. I could not have cared less, however. At last I was my own woman with my own home and my own income, small though it might be. The only drawback was that I was getting a bit tired of purely female company, much as I loved the girls' nights at May and Meg's. But at the age of forty, what chance was there of meeting any Mister, let alone Mister Right? Soon a solution presented itself. Ever one to tell myself, 'Don't just stand there, do something,' I picked up a copy of a local free newspaper *The Tyneside Champion* one night and saw with interest that they had a 'Lonely Hearts' section. Well why not, I thought, it's worth a try.

5

After buying a copy of the paper, my first task was to look at the adverts put in by male readers and I tried to think what sort of person I might like to meet. About my own age would be good. Solvent, yes, but not necessarily rich. After all, any money a rich man might have would be his, and I had finished with being reliant on anyone else, so as long as he had a reasonably secure job with perhaps some prospects, that would do for me. A car owner would be nice for outings, and someone who shared at least some of my own interests. Most definitely someone who did not play the field or drink to excess, I had had enough of both. Character and personality were important: loyal, dependable, not given to emotional outbursts … oh dear! The list was endless. Did such a paragon exist? Well, I would find out.

So I scanned the adverts, made my choice, and replied to one or two. Replies were sent to the newspaper using the reference number of each advert, and from there were forwarded to the advertiser, thus ensuring anonymity. I sat back and waited … but nothing happened. Not a sausage. This was definitely not going to work, so pen in hand, I prepared an advert of my own. I gave my age, said I was a widow, and that I was looking for companionship with someone of about my own age with similar interests, which I listed as country walks, cinema, reading and outings. Before long replies began to arrive, bundled together in one large envelope by the newspaper. I was amazed. This really worked, and what fun it was opening up each envelope and wondering what it might contain.

One of the first that I opened obviously thought that he just *had* to be the man of my dreams, as he told me very little about himself, but in great detail said where and when we should meet the following evening. That one went straight in the bin.

There were two who, although a little younger than me, were divorced men and both sounded like quite decent fellows. As I did not have a phone at that time, making arrangements meant walking up the street to the nearest phone box, which could be a task in itself depending on how long the queue was to use it, or even worse if it was out of order at the time, necessitating a hike to the other end of the road. Anyhow, I made arrangements to meet two of my applicants on consecutive nights at the local pub.

Poor fellows, I felt quite sorry for them. Both had suffered traumatic divorces with wives clearing off and leaving the children to be raised by the husband's parents. They were both, it seemed, looking for a replacement to look after the children, but with a family of my own as well as a job I enjoyed, this was just not going to happen, so regretfully I thanked them for my glass of shandy and bid them farewell outside the pub.

The next one claimed to be 45 and sounded quite promising. He asked to meet me at the bus station so that we could go out for the day one Saturday. We duly met up and took the bus to Hexham, and after tea at a café we went to stroll around the lovely park near the town. It was a hot day and as we sat on the grass I could feel my face starting to burn as my skin does not take kindly to the sun. Although he had claimed to be 45 he was at least 10 years older than that and his dentist had done him no favours when he fitted his false teeth as they clacked alarmingly when he talked. He was obviously trying to make an effort and when I told him of my children he coyly said that no doubt they would know him. Somewhat puzzled, I asked him what he meant and it transpired that he ran a joke shop in a rundown part of the town. It was with some relief that we parted.

The next two after that were without doubt married men on the make and after one outing each I called it a day. One took me to a nightclub which really was not my cup of tea, and the other had, in my opinion, seen better days.

So I tried another advert and this time I met an Indian doctor. He was very nice and we went out quite a few times, mainly because I liked his expensive car, but his main topic of conversation was his thwarted love affair with a lady when he was practising in Northallerton, so I soon got fed up with that and stopped meeting him.

Then I met Bob, a bit younger than me and, he said, separated from his wife. As by then, I had pretty well given up any hope of finding a lifetime partner, I was happy to go out with him from time to time as he was great fun to be with. Often he would take me and Cathleen down to the coast for a picnic. I made no demands on him as I was quite content with my life at that time, and on his part I think he was quite fond of me, so it worked for both of us and certainly made life more interesting.

At work the whole system ground to a halt that summer as the Royal Mail staged a nationwide strike and no post was delivered. As the bulk of our work came through the mail, it wasn't too long before all the tidying up had been done and all we could do was sit around and look at each other, as the system was not set up to take phone calls. One of the girls who worked on our section, also called Pat, was quite a character. Recently divorced and childless, she adopted all the latest fashions, including probably the first set of hot pants seen in the north-east. When she walked down the main corridors the men would flock out of the side offices to watch her go past in her raspberry-pink, tight-fitting shorts. She loved it, and so did they!

Finally, as the postal strike wore on, it was decided that we should come into work every other day.

Having achieved CO status I was keen to go further, but

this usually meant a long wait before hopefully being selected to go for a board. There was a scheme by which, as with the CO grade, an exam could be taken, but it was only open to under 25s. To my joy, however, a circular came around saying that that restriction had been lifted, and the exam would be open to anyone. I would have to complete my year's probationary period as a CO, but meanwhile later next year I would be able to sign up for a further course of night classes to prepare myself for the next step.

I still visited Maryon as often as possible. She was gradually reducing Woodburn to a similar state to that in which she had left St Mary's Mount. Maryon never did any housework but spent her time raising her dogs and selling them. By then she had reached the age of 80, and while her sister Ethel had opted to pay into the National Insurance scheme at its inception, Maryon had decided to have no truck with it, a decision she probably regretted when she saw her sister happily collecting her pension every week. Now, however, under an additional pension scheme, anyone who had never paid National Insurance could claim a small pension at the age of 80. I got the claim forms for her and helped her fill them in and she was cock-a-hoop to receive a reduced but regular amount each week.

When visiting her one night, I asked her what had happened to the cottage. Dene Cottage in Nenthead, a village in the hills above Alston, had been a feature in our family life down the years. Originally it had been bought shortly after the First World War by my grandfather's sister, Great-aunt Allie, who with her husband, Uncle Jim, would travel up there regularly until he died in 1936. Maryon, who also had a wooden bungalow over in the next valley on the way to Allenheads, had bought it from her in the late 1930s and we had often stayed there for holidays, especially during the war when the coastline was denied to us. It had been built in the late 1600s with the living quarters on the first floor

61

reached by a wide stone staircase, while downstairs had been intended to house the livestock during the winter. It had two advantages: electricity, and running water with waterborne sewerage. The toilet was housed in a wooden structure filled with spiders in the dark undercroft while alongside was a separate section with double doors that had housed Great-aunt Allie's little Austin 30 runabout. The top of the stone stairs widened out into a small terrace and the front door led straight into the living room. To the left was a small room with a sink, a cold water tap, and on a rickety table a two-plate electric cooker. Beyond was space for a single bed. On the other side of the living room was the bedroom, while heating was provided by the fireplace in the living room.

Years ago, when Ron and I had first been married and Anne was a baby, we had lived there for a while until my father's estate was settled, Ron got a job with the Division of Atomic Energy and we had moved to Warrington and bought a house. So now I fell to wondering what had happened to it. It seemed that because it had been standing empty for some years, the local council had been trying to contact Maryon, unsuccessfully, for some time. Lacking any response, they had told her that they intended to put a demolition order on it and that she would have to bear the cost of pulling it down. Typically for Maryon she had chosen to ignore this, but it seemed that it worried her somewhat.

I gave it some thought, as I had a great fondness for the place, and finally asked her if she would mind if I had a look to see what could be done. She was happy to take me up on my suggestion, so one day when I had one of our bonus days off, Bob drove me up into the hills and into the village of Nenthead. What a wonderful sight it was as we came over the shoulder of the hills and looked down on the village nestling below us. So many memories returned as I took my first sight of it after some 20 years.

The keys to the cottage were always held by Betty, who lived in a large farmhouse across the road with her husband, Harris, and whom I had known most of my life. She was delighted to see me and we caught up with all our news. When Ron and I had lived there, her children had been in their early teens. She had two boys and a girl, now all grown-up and she was sorry to hear of Ron's death. Her daughter, Margaret, had trained as a nurse and gone to live and work in Australia where sadly it was discovered that she had inoperable cancer. Betty and her younger son, Alan, flew out to be with her during her last days and they stayed at a local guest house run by a lady and her daughter Mary. During their extended stay, Mary and Alan fell in love. After his return to England, Alan and Mary kept in touch and the plan was for Mary to come to England and she and Alan would be married here in Nenthead. Betty's elder son was courting a lady who was divorced with a young child, but Betty was happy for them and treated the little boy as a grandson.

The farmhouse where she lived was just as I remembered it. The front door was rarely used and the side door always stood open as it led into what had been her father-in-law's shop during the years when he was the village cobbler. In fact, during the war he had made me a pair of clogs which I remembered as being the most comfortable footwear I had ever possessed. Now he was long dead, all his tools still gathered dust on the shelves, but the counter did duty for the sale of the eggs that Alan collected from his battery hens in the big sheds higher up the valley.

After all our catching up, Betty hunted out the keys for me – no mean feat – and Bob and I climbed the stone stairs and opened the front door of the cottage. Inside little had changed although all the furniture had gone. It seemed that at one point Maryon had rented it out to a local couple, but they had been evicted when they failed to pay the rent. The inside was dry and there was no smell of rot or damp. Being in the building trade, Bob gave it a good going over for me and announced that he could see nothing wrong with the walls or the roof, and that all things considered it was in good condition.

The manner in which it was sited was quite unusual and I could only think that in years gone by it had stood alone, facing south and with the small stream running nearby. Later on, lead was discovered in the surrounding hills and the Quakers had started mining there and built cottages for their workers in the village, so that at the rear of the cottage, a row of back-to-back dwellings had been built on. When Ron and I had lived there we had stripped the walls of layers of wallpaper and found a blocked-up window in the rear wall where the newer buildings had been joined on. As Bob pointed out, this meant that any updating of the building would have to take into account some cross-ventilation as all the current windows faced to the front of the building. Satisfied with what we had found, we returned the key to Betty and after buying some of Alan's lovely fresh eggs, drove back to Newcastle.

There were other things afoot at that time. Schemes were in place to help to upgrade much of the older run-down property in the country, and 50 per cent grants were available for renovation work to be done. I thought that I might be able to benefit from such a scheme, but first I had to discuss the situation with Maryon. She was more than happy for me to take the place off her hands, as there was no way she could bring it up to date herself and in the course of time it would be bound to fall into further disrepair. So she agreed to make it over to me by a deed of gift and the wheels were set in motion with the solicitor.

I then got in touch with the local council offices in Alston. At that time, council affairs had yet to be amalgamated into large concerns and so I agreed to meet the Clerk of the

Council up in Alston. I decided to take the train there, so on the agreed day I went to Newcastle Central Station to catch the Carlisle train. It was a beautiful early spring day and the train was relatively empty, so I was able to have a seat next to the window. We soon left the city behind and wended our way up the Tyne valley, where now and again the train would cross the river as it gurgled happily along the bottom of the rich and fertile valley floor. Here and there the river was edged by trees now in their early spring freshness, while a light breeze stirred the branches and the sun shining through the leaves dappled the lush green meadows.

After a stop at Hexham, we climbed higher into the hills until we reached a place called Haltwhistle where I alighted and waited on the deserted platform in the pale spring sunshine for the little local train to Alston. When it came trundling down the tracks it was but a single carriage and I was one of the few passengers along with a young man with a clipboard. Later I realised he was there to count the number of people using the train as the line was under threat of closure, and in fact, at a later date, despite local objections the line did close. But on that beautiful day I drank in the passing scenery as we trundled across the high bridge at Staward Peel and I gazed far down at the tumbling stream in the depths of the valley.

Alston was the end of the line, and climbing out I made my way up the steep incline to the town and up the main street to the Town Hall. There I found the Town Clerk and together we drove in his car to Nenthead and the cottage. The landscape was quite different from the Tyne valley as we drove along the narrow roads bordered by dry stone walls, while behind them the hills swept up to heather-clad tops. Reaching Nenthead we turned off into the little village street and over the bridge until we came to the left-hand turn which brought us to the front of the cottage.

Although the spring sunshine brightened up the aspect,

still it could not hide the general run-down feeling of the building as a whole. Paint was peeling off the woodwork, the doors that led to what had been used as a garage by my great-aunt Allie were now in danger of coming off their hinges, and the stone work looked as if it would benefit from a good scrub.

Nevertheless, inside was as dry and sweet-smelling as ever and the Town Clerk agreed with me that it would be a suitable subject for renovation. After making some suggestions he said I should submit plans and the council would give me their decision. As it appeared that this would be the first building to benefit from the new regulations in the area, he was quite keen for me to do it so that others might be encouraged to do the same. However, I said that while it would be great to have the grant, I myself had no money, but would be looking for a council loan to cover the rest. That, he said, would be no problem. After he had dropped me back in Alston I had lunch at the local hotel then made my way to the station for my return journey.

One spin-off from the postal strike was that when it was over we had such a backlog of claims to clear that there was overtime available for all who wanted it. Unable to take advantage of as much as I would have liked, I managed several evenings and was able to amass £50 to pay back half of what I had borrowed from Maryon. However, Pat, she of the hot pants, worked evenings and weekends for as long as the overtime lasted and saved up enough to put down a deposit on a modest little terraced house in Gosforth. Not just a pretty face, our Pat.

Meanwhile, Christopher had graduated from the junior to the senior school which was a newish sixties building further up Benton Road. He told me that he got some bullying about his accent, which while not being exactly South African was certainly not native Geordie-speak. My tenant upstairs had told me that once or twice Christopher had come home and scaled the back wall, staying out there for the day, so it seemed that things were not going too well for him at school. I was concerned as at that time the more sympathetic term 'one parent family' had yet to be coined, and I worried that if the powers that be felt I was unable to control my children, steps might be taken against me, especially if he played truant on a regular basis. But mainly, of course, his education was paramount when it came to any expectations for his future.

On Parents' Day I went along and expressed my concerns. The school promised they would look into it and if he was being bullied, they would take care of it. Additionally, I said I was worried about his spelling and about the fact that in South Africa they had thought he might be suffering from dyslexia. To my astonishment I got the response that 'We don't really worry about spelling as long as the sense is there'! I couldn't have been more shocked. It was not so long before that our essays were marked with a rigid respect for spelling, while earlier still regular spelling tests were the order of the day. However could our lovely language continue to be written, or indeed understood, if spelling was neglected? It seemed that standards were no longer what they once were.

During that summer I not only reached my fortieth birthday, but it was also now five years since Ron had died so suddenly. Looking back it was hard to understand how I had managed to deal with those terrible years. Only someone who has lost their soulmate can know how devastating it is to be virtually torn in two emotionally and left stunned from the sudden wrenching away of the person who was part of oneself. Added to which was the heavy responsibility of becoming both mother and father to four children in a land so far away from the country of my birth. Without parents, brothers or sisters, there was little advice or support to be had, but with God's help I had finally reached a plateau of, if not content, at least of security and the hope of some sort of future. I could count my blessings, my only regret being my run-in with Louie who had taken advantage of my vulnerable state. But not any more. No one would ever do that to me again.

I still met up with Joe every lunchtime and as we took our walk I was able to discuss with him so many factors which affected both our lives. I have heard it said that there is no such thing as a platonic friendship between a man and a woman, but over the years I have been blessed and privileged to have several, and Joe was one of the best.

I had had very little contact with my mother- and father-in-law who had moved back and forth to the UK more than once. As the pensions increased and she was unable to benefit from them, my mother-in-law would pack up and return to England. On one famous occasion their goods never left the docks before she changed her mind and went back to South Africa. On another occasion they had bought a mobile home in Surrey and seemed to enjoy that for some time before packing up once more.

It is sometimes difficult to change countries. There is always the hankering after the place of one's birth, and yet the new country also holds much to be admired. For myself I felt no tugging of the heartstrings for South Africa and was content to remake my life in England, but for my two eldest children England left a lot to be desired, and who could blame them. Their introduction to this country had been to north-east England during a particularly cold January, so it was hardly surprising that they were unsettled.

That summer, Ron's elder sister, Margery, and her husband Bram were in England on furlough from South Africa, courtesy of the Salvation Army, and were staying with Bram's sister Ruby in her large house in the West End of Newcastle. They contacted me one day to ask if I would have their younger son Stephen to stay while they took a trip to Belgium.

I was only too happy to do so as I was very fond of the lad who was about 12 or 13 at the time. So we squeezed up the boys in their large front bedroom and they all enjoyed each other's company. It had been Bram and Margery's appointment to South Africa in the early 1950s that had resulted in us deciding to emigrate ourselves. His younger sister Miriam and her husband Ronnie were still living there but his younger brother Tom and his wife Iris had returned to the UK and had bought a newsagent and sweetshop near Cheltenham from where Iris had originated. However there was very little contact with us and Cathleen was not even aware that she had grandparents. It seemed pointless to tell her, as my mother-in-law never wrote to any of the children or remembered their birthdays. It seemed to me that with the death of her son, her interest in me or the children ceased. My father-in-law was a wonderful man of whom I was very fond, but my mother-in-law had never had much time for me.

Stephen was a very clever boy who had always lived in the shadow of his older brother, Bramwell. Young Bramwell had been born with a tendency to terrible eczema, and as a baby not only could fish not even be brought into the house without him breaking into terrible weeping sores, but at night time his arms had to be put into cardboard splints and tied to the sides of the cot to prevent him scratching himself into a bleeding wreck. Consequently he grew up needing much of his mother's attention and when poor Stephen came along, while he was not exactly neglected, Bramwell's needs were always paramount. Stephen meanwhile quietly got on with his life and at one time set up internal telephones all around their house, while his Meccano models were a sight to behold. He was very welcome and I think he enjoyed his stay with my two boys.

At last the solicitor finalised the deed of gift of the cottage from Maryon to me. Meanwhile I had been drawing up the plans for the alterations I wanted to make. House plans had always held an attraction for me and had I been better at maths I would have liked to have become an architect. The council had said they would be happy to look at any ideas I cared to put forward, so I sketched out what I envisaged as well as I could. Downstairs the enclosed end room, which had been used as a garage, would become the kitchen with a window let in to the side wall to allow for cross-ventilation. At the back of the room on the left a door would be broken through into the large undercroft which would become the living room. The door which presently gave access into that room from outside would be partly bricked up to form a window and a further window would be let into the wall at the far end of the house. Back in the kitchen the large garage doors would be taken off and the wall filled in, leaving space for a glass outer door letting in more light An open staircase would rise up the left-hand wall to a corridor running along the back of the cottage and at the top to the right would be another small window let into the end wall, a bathroom on the right above the kitchen and an electric immersion heater in the cupboard above the stairwell. At the other end of the corridor a door would lead into the smaller bedroom, which had once been the kitchen, the front window being blocked up and a new window set into the end wall. The main bedroom, which used to be the living room, would open off the corridor but have the fireplace removed. I retained the front door opening onto the little stone balcony, however, as well as keeping the stone stairs.

I sent off the plans and before long had them passed. I was sent a list of local builders, as at least three quotes had to be produced under the terms of the grant system. One builder was out of my league as they dealt with very high-class renovations, so it was no surprise to receive an extremely high quote from them. Of the other two, the most reasonable was from a firm of two brothers who did a lot of local work and this was the one I preferred. They were all sent off to the council and the job finally went to the two brothers.

The council had said they would like to have the roof

replaced, as no one could be sure of the state of the timbers underneath. I felt sad about that as it was made of large stone slabs and it would be replaced by a man-made fabric. Although this would look quite nice it would take away a lot of the character of the cottage, but this was a time before so much emphasis was put on preserving original features, so I went along with it. No doubt the builders made a bob or two out of selling the stone slabs.

As Christmas approached the roof had been renewed – of course the timbers had been in perfect condition – and the big tasks of filling in the doorways and putting in the new windows had been completed before the winter weather descended upon the hills. On the roads in the surrounding hills, high wooden poles lined the sides so that when the snow drifted, the roadway could still be made out, when or if the snow ploughs could get through; winter weather was no laughing matter at those heights. Alston was said to be the highest market town in England, and Nenthead was higher again, so winter weather was taken seriously.

The work was progressing satisfactorily, and yet to be honest I had no idea how I would pay for it when it was all finished, let alone furnish the place or even how to get there myself without a car. I just knew it was something I had to do and that somehow it would all work out.

That September Cathleen had left the nursery class and moved up to the first-year reception class, but things weren't working out too well. The teacher was a young woman just out of training college and somewhat out of her depth with 30-odd children to teach. Cathleen made no bones about her dislike of the new arrangement, showing her feelings by leaving the class and running back screaming to the nursery class. They had been so good to her there and it had been through the dedicated efforts of the nursery teacher that she had finally begun to talk properly. I went to see the headmistress and we discussed the problem, but there was little that could be done except to hope that Cathleen would eventually settle in, which after a while she seemed to do.

I knew that she must be suffering developmental problems and although I had run the gamut of specialists and various tests, I had been left with no conclusion or even a diagnosis as to what might be the problem. Physically she had developed very well, but I felt there had been a halt in her progress at the time of her father's death when she was only fourteen months old. At that point she had begun to say 'Mama' and 'Dada' and to prattle away in a babyish manner, but all that seemed to have come to a halt when we had to move to the Girls' Home in Johannesburg. She was bright, however, and always knew what she wanted. In point of fact, at times she had a will of iron, but somehow there seemed to be something missing and she was making no progress at school, although admittedly these were early days. There seemed to be little that could be done, so I could only hope that with time things would improve.

As Christmas came and went I began to realise the drawbacks of dating a married man, as of course, although separated from his wife, Bob spent the holiday period with his family. I had enjoyed our relationship and to some extent he had helped to heal the bruised feelings left from my encounter with Louie, but now I felt it was time to move on, so in the New Year I sent off another advertisement to *The Tyneside Champion*. Again several replies turned up, a couple of them once more married men looking for some fun, which was patently obvious on the first and only meeting. I was tired of short-lived arrangements and felt I needed to find someone a bit more committed and permanent.

Two letters came through at the same time. One was from a man who said he was a solicitor living in Chester-le-Street. The other, when I opened it up, struck me at once, for it began:

Dear lady of the 'Life begins at forty' . . .

6

Alex was, he said, a 'young' 44-year-old man who had been on his own for the last four years and divorced for just over two of them. He drove a two-year-old car which would be replaced by his firm later that year. His address, which he gave, was in Gosforth, a nice suburb just north of Newcastle where he lived on his own but where his mother came once a month to make sure he was keeping his flat clean. He spent most evenings working at home but had Sunday lunch at his mother's every week. Suggesting we should meet and talk, he said he would quite understand should I not wish to see him again after meeting up, it would be entirely my choice.

His whole letter, while not too well written, rang with sincerity and he had suggested a time and place where he would wait on the next two Fridays. I knew that this was one person I really would like to meet. Not only that but the letters from the newspaper had arrived that morning, a Friday, and I read them after I had come home from work. Never one to rein in my impulses, I realised that if I left straight after our evening meal I could with luck arrive at the meeting place, outside an antique shop on the corner of Gosforth High Street, by the designated time. I would have to walk to the end of Chillingham Road, a fair distance, then catch a bus which would take me to Gosforth. After we had eaten, I set off without delay.

The bus seemed to take forever to wind its way towards Gosforth, and as I alighted at the stop near the High Street the street lights glimmered softly through the gloom and reflected damply on the roads and pavements. Approaching the corner, I saw a figure standing gazing into the window of the antique shop and knew this must be the man I had come to meet. Before he was aware of my presence, I had time to see that he was taller than me and looked well-dressed in an army-type winter coat and a hat. As I slowly approached, he looked round and when I hesitatingly approached him, he turned said, 'Hello, are you the lady I wrote to?'

I replied that I was. As I looked at him and saw blue eyes, nice even features and a kindly expression, I knew without a shadow of doubt that here was a man I could trust. We introduced ourselves and he suggested that we should walk to a nearby pub so that we could talk undisturbed. Once settled down, Alex told me that he had one daughter who was 20 and lived with her mother. He worked as a salesman for a company called Armour, quite well known at that time for the corned beef they imported from Argentina. This part of the business had suffered greatly from an outbreak of food poisoning from some of its meat products and the company was attempting to get by with selling cans of fruit, vegetables and baked beans. For most of the week he was out visiting stores and butcher's shops in Northumberland, down into Durham and along the north-east coast, chasing up orders for canned goods. It was hard work and his only outing, apart from his visit to his mother every Sunday, was an evening spent with a friend who lived not too far from me near the Coast Road.

On his divorce the family home had been sold and Alex had ensured that his ex-wife received half of the proceeds of the sale, at a time when this was not yet law. He said that from the start he had realised that he and his ex-wife had not been suited, and that he had spent some time back in the regular army serving as a sergeant-major in the military police in Cyprus during the problems they had had in that country.

I told him something of my own history and it transpired that he had bought a similar pair of flats to mine, except that his was an upstairs flat not far from where we were sitting.

As a child of eight he had had an accident that had infected the area behind his kneecap, the treatment for which was complete immobilisation of his leg in plaster-of-paris from hip to toes, which had prevented him from attending school. It was more than a year before the plaster was removed but of course in the meantime the muscles on his leg had withered and it was to be a further two years before he returned to school at the age of 11. This explained why his letter was not too well written. To compound this interruption to his education, when war broke out most of the teachers at his school were mobilised into the forces and he had left at 14 without any qualifications.

Alex had grown up in a mining village, his father being a miner, so in those days and in that area a child who was not considered to be fit enough to go down the mines tended to be ignored. During the war, however, he had risen to the rank of sergeant in the military police and had been part of the International Patrol that policed Vienna in the days after the war.

His father had died some years before at a time when his parents were running a social club in a village just north of Newcastle. This meant that his mother had had to vacate the premises and for some years she had divided her time between his home and that of his sister, Irene. She had worked in the Gentlemen's Bar of the County Hotel in Gosforth where she had met Alex's stepfather, Ossie Clark. They had now been married for a few years and lived in a bungalow in Gosforth.

Not all of this came up on that first meeting however, but after I had taken Alex to my home and introduced him to the family. We would spend those winter evenings either in a pub somewhere, out having a meal, or visiting May and Meg or Maryon.

One night, not long after Alex and I had met, I came out from work with my friend Agnes and found Bob waiting for me. I apologised to Agnes and said I would be getting a lift home. Good soul that he was, Bob wondered why he had not heard from me, but when I told him I had met someone, and it might be serious, he was pleased for me and said that he had realised that he would not have been able to hold on to me for much longer. After wishing me all the best for the future, he dropped me off at home.

I had told Alex of my daily walks with Joe, so one lunchtime, as Joe and I set off down the road, Alex was waiting at the corner to meet us. I gladly introduced Joe and the three of us strolled around chatting until it was time to return. It was obvious that Alex wanted to ensure that there was no 'funny business' going on behind his back, which I quite understood and which didn't bother me as I had nothing to hide.

I can only imagine what his mother must have felt when he told her that he had met a widow with four children! But before long I was taken to meet her and her husband Ossie. I found them to be lovely people and most welcoming, whatever their underlying doubts might have been. I have seldom met anyone with such a strong sense of fairness as Annie, she ensured that all her family were treated equally, with no favourites. She had been very upset by her son's divorce and, I suspect, harboured hopes that they would get back together again. But the divorce had been very bitter, even though no third parties had been involved. Nonetheless, after we had met, she told me later that she had been to see Jenny, to tell her of the development, perhaps in the hope that it might not be too late to repair their marriage. But that was never going to happen. I did not hold it against her as she thought she was doing the best for her son.

Ossie came from a family of four. He had been a widower when he met Annie but he and his first wife had had no children. He and his brother had run the family printing firm and the two sisters Ciss and Jess, both childless widows, lived nearby. Eventually I met them all. Later we travelled down to Blyth where Alex's sister Irene and her husband Dave ran a pub called The Market in the town centre. Dave had been a miner too but after an accident at the mine, when some of his friends were badly injured, he had left and he and Irene were trained by the brewery at another pub. Here their daughter, Anne, met her husband Jim, the son of the licensees. Their young son, David, was currently at school at the Gosforth High School.

It was good to start going out together on a regular basis. At the weekends, if the weather wasn't too bad, we would drive out into the surrounding countryside or to the coast. I loved the run up to places like Bamborough Castle and the stupendous Northumberland landscape and I found that we had a similar love of exploring old churches and cathedrals, castles and museums. Durham Cathedral was always a pleasure, with a walk around the base of the hill alongside the river with the cathedral soaring above. I enjoyed being part of a couple once more and Cathleeen loved going with us wherever we decided to go.

One Saturday evening, Alex took me to the Park Hotel at Tynemouth for an evening meal; at that time the hotel was what we would call 'upmarket'. As we drove home, we discussed seriously the idea of making this permanent. There was much to think about, but I knew that here was a man I could trust and we had the same views and outlook on life. His birthday fell on St Patrick's Day, March 17th, so as a celebration I asked him if I could take him to the Five Bridges Hotel in Gateshead for a meal.

If the Park Hotel had been good, the Five Bridges was magnificent. It was somewhere I had always wanted to go and now seemed a good opportunity. I took £5 with me, a lot of money in those days, and we had a splendid lobster soup to start with. I didn't quite know what to do when the waiter poured some brandy in it and then set it alight! Was I supposed to douse the flames, or just let it burn? The rest of the meal lived up to the same high standards, but when it was time to settle the bill, horror of horrors, my £5 was not enough and I had to quietly ask Alex to help me out. Fortunately that did not spell the end of our romance!

The winter days dragged on and I was able to tell Alex about the cottage and the work that had been started on it, so one lovely day in early spring we set off with Cathleen to drive west beyond Hexham and up into the hills. Knowing the route well, I showed Alex the way and we were able to enjoy the changing landscape as we left Hexham and the cultivated valleys, heading up over the moors with their endless stone walls stretching over the hill tops. Eventually we breasted the final hill and dropped down into the head of the valley where the village of Nenthead nestled. Turning off the main road to the left we drove down the narrow village street past the pub on the right and made the sharp left turn which brought us to the front of the cottage. Alex stopped the car and turned off the engine.

As we opened the doors, the car was filled with the fresh country air and we stepped out to hear the slight breeze sighing through the pine trees higher up the valley. Together we walked to the little footbridge over the rushing stream that came down from the hills, while above us we could hear the call of the curlews and the distant cry of the sheep. Otherwise all was silence and we drank in the atmosphere before turning to look at the cottage. I could see that the new window let into this gable end of the cottage would have a view all the way up the valley and over the surrounding hills. As this was to be the kitchen, washing up was never going to be a chore.

It seemed that the main outer structural changes had been completed. There was the new roof, and the new doors and windows were all exactly in place just as I had envisaged them. We peered through the downstairs windows but it was obvious that none of the internal work had been started yet so we walked across to Betty's where we received a warm welcome and I was able to introduce her to Alex. After enjoying a cup of tea with her, we bought some of the lovely fresh eggs before reluctantly leaving for the long drive back to Newcastle.

During our long talks together Alex let me know his intentions were serious; as he put it, 'It was all or nothing.' I knew that educationally I had many more advantages than he had had. I also knew that he was not a great conversationalist, but I remember thinking to myself one lunchtime as I walked to meet Joe, 'Well, conversation I can find wherever I go, but a good man is hard to find.' Most importantly though, I knew that we both had a strong sense of commitment, and that as we had both known some hard times, we were ready to settle down together and make a life for ourselves.

I had realised fairly early on in my widowhood that one day I would want to marry again, but an incident I had witnessed while I was running the Young Women's Hostel in Johannesburg had made me realise that not all marriages were the same. There was a parking garage opposite the hostel in Kerk Street, and as I idly looked out of my bedroom window one day, I watched a young couple with a baby arrive at the garage to collect their car. The wife waited with the baby in the pram surrounded by their shopping while the husband brought the car down. He then leapt out, loaded all the shopping into the boot while his wife looked on, then handed her the baby out of the pram and raced about folding it and placing it in with the shopping before opening the passenger door and carefully assisting her in. Quite a tender scene, and yet I knew that if it had been me, I would have had the child safely tucked under my arm while, with the other hand I folded the pram. I would have let him lift the pram into the car, but I would have been there picking up parcels and handing them to him. There was no way I could have stood to one side and played the helpless female!

My run-in with Louie had been an eye-opener. I had gone into the relationship with high expectations of loyalty and commitment, only to be landed with a control freak and a serial adulterer, so I needed a great deal of assurance before I could really trust again. I read a quote one day which went something like this:

How quickly your life can change: a day, an hour,
And all the hours flowing from that, weeks, months ...
    years.

Was that how it would be for us?

I had a letter from the builders asking what I wanted doing in the kitchen. After talking it over with Alex, we came across an advertisement for an entirely new concept in England, a fitted kitchen which could be bought cheaply in flat packs and installed in situ. The name of the company was MFI and while the ordering could be done by mail they had opened up premises in Wembley where the goods could be seen.

It transpired that Alex's company car was due for exchange and Armour asked if he would be prepared to drive it down to London and pick up the replacement, so this seemed to be an excellent opportunity to kill several birds with one stone. As well as the car exchange we could go to Wembley and see about the kitchen cupboards and at the same time call in on Anne where she was living in a bedsit in Croydon, so that she and Alex could meet.

We travelled overnight. The journey down was tedious as the new motorway did not go the whole way to London, but eventually we arrived in the early morning and found the address where Anne had a bedsit, shared I had no doubt with her boyfriend Dave.

After we had announced our arrival on the intercom it took some time for the communal outside door to be opened, but soon we climbed up a couple of flights to the small room where she was living. After settling ourselves down, surprise, surprise, Dave suddenly appeared at the door carrying a sports bag. I realised that we were to assume that he did not live here but had just popped in on his way somewhere else. Stifling my giggles, I wondered if he thought we had come to sort him out for living with my daughter, and so I quickly introduced Alex and produced the bacon and eggs that he had suggested we buy at a local shop. A substantial breakfast soon put us all at ease and we explained that we intended to travel over to Wembley to look at the fitted kitchens.

We decided to go by train as Alex was quite familiar with the underground system, and eventually we alighted at Wembley station and made our way to the nearby industrial estate where MFI was situated. We found the huge warehouse where there was a hum of activity, with young besuited men busily demonstrating the goods and taking orders. We finally found the kitchen section where kitchens had been set up to show the finished product, and there was one which would just suit us. It was made from a laminated product which looked remarkably like wood and was quite narrow, unlike later models which were a standard size. This was just right for our narrow little kitchen and producing the plan and the measurements which we had brought with us, we selected a range of wall and floor units.

We then had another hurdle to climb. The advertisement we had seen, and brought with us, stated that the purchase could be paid for in instalments, as needless to say there was no cash available to pay for the whole lot. However, we were told that items purchased on the premises had to be paid for there and then. Naturally we objected, considering how far we had come to buy from them. It also seemed a strange way to do business. Several of the suited young man were called over and after a rather brisk exchange we were given the monthly payment scheme. Delivery was to be to the builders in Alston, and after giving the address we left to make our way back to Anne. After saying our farewells, we set off back to Newcastle once more, well satisfied with our trip.

There was one thing over which we were never going to agree, and that was my driving. One day Alex had asked me if I would like to drive the car. Willingly I changed seats with him but it was immediately obvious that he intended to treat me as a learner driver whom he would have to teach. After some miles of instructions to 'change down now', 'don't drive so near to the kerb', I stopped the car and pointed out to him that I was an experienced driver, having driven for over 20 years at that time, and also that I had passed three driving tests, two in England and one in South Africa. He, by contrast, had learned to drive in the army and on his discharge had been given a driving licence without the necessity of taking a test. Nothing I said ever made any difference, so for the majority of our lives together I refused to drive while he was in the car with me as it always left me speechless with rage! Other than that, we had no differences.

Soon the builders had completed their work on the cottage, so we purchased camp beds and borrowed a two-burner cooker from Irene until such time as we could afford to buy an electric cooker. Thus armed, we drove up to Nenthead every Friday night loaded down with step-ladders and white paint for the interior. Once the painting was done, Alex measured up the space alongside the old chimney breast in the new bedroom and made a fitted wardrobe. I made curtains of light flowery material and draped a fine net across the upper door in the bedroom, so that on fine nights the door could be left open to the clean cool air.

One of the girls I worked with on Family Allowances told me she had a cousin who was selling some bunk beds, so we went down to see them. They were of good solid construction so we bought them for the small second bedroom where Cathleen could sleep in comfort. Alex also built another small wardrobe in that room and a shelf as a dressing table.

A friend of May's, who often came to our girls' nights, offered us a three-piece suite from her home that had belonged to her mother-in-law. Anxious at last to have some furniture of her own choice, she was only too glad to give it to us, so it sat in over-stuffed splendour in our new lounge. Bit by bit that summer, our dream cottage took shape and at the same time we grew closer together, until at last it was time to decide on our future.

But before we made any arrangements there was one more thing I had to do. I had managed to save a further £50 and I repaid Auntie Maryon the balance of the £100 she had loaned me to help me to buy the flat in which I lived.

With my debts paid we concluded our plans, and chose August 2nd 1971 for our wedding.

7

Ideally, both of us would have liked to have been married in church, but at that time divorced people were not encouraged to make their vows in the Church of England. I of course, had no problem being a widow, but as Alex was a divorcee I had no wish to go cap-in-hand to various churches looking for one which would deign to marry us.

However, the new Civic Centre, known locally as 'Dan's Palace' after Dan Smith of the later Poulson scandal fame, had an impressive wedding suite where we could be married by the Registrar. So we made our plans and invited all the family. Anne and her boyfriend Dave travelled up from London, and my eldest son Paul and Alex's daughter Jacqueline were our witnesses. The service was quiet and meaningful as we made our promises surrounded by our families, while the wedding breakfast was a modest one of cakes and sandwiches supplied by a local baker and served in my flat. Money was short and none was to be wasted on an elaborate 'do'.

Needless to say our honeymoon was spent at the cottage, with glorious days out on the moors or driving across the hills to the Eden Valley, Carlisle and beyond. Cathleen was left behind to stay with relatives, although until the last moment we had thought to take her with us, then the generous offer was made. I felt a deep sense of happiness as I looked at my new wedding ring and at the kindly man seated next to me in the car. Already we had worked hard together to complete the cottage and I was optimistic for our future together.

At lunchtime on the last day at work before leaving for my wedding, our section had taken me down to the local pub to celebrate. Never a big drinker, I had several large sherries so was feeling no pain as we stumbled back to the office. Hardly was I seated at my desk before I was summoned to the HEO's office. After congratulating me on my impending nuptials, he told me that on my return I would be transferred to a new section that was being set up in the main buildings. The plan was to put all the Family Allowance details onto the computer, the first department to be so treated. We had wondered why young men with stopwatches had been timing us as we awarded new claims, and now we knew. It was expected that the job would take over a year, so somewhat sobered I returned to our office to tell them the news. It seemed that a few people were being taken from each section as people with experience of the benefit were needed to undertake the work.

So after our honeymoon and on my return to work I went back to my old section to say goodbye and to collect my personal belongings before walking back up to the main building to find and report to the room where the clerical work would be done. To my delight I found that Agnes was to join me there as well. We were housed in a huge room lined by desks in groups of six, and Agnes and I soon claimed places next to each other. When all were gathered together we were told that the plan was to transfer all the details of every child in the country from the old ledger sheets onto computerised forms which would then be taken to the machine operators to install into the new system. This, we were told, while remarkably simple work, needed to be done at Clerical Officer grade because finance was involved. Each section's ledgers would be brought up in batches, the sheets taken out of the folders and all the information on the parents, their addresses, the children's names and their dates of birth would be transcribed onto specially prepared sheets, making it a simple job for the machinists to input it all onto the computers.

And so we started, day after day of mind-bogglingly simple tasks which left us plenty of time to talk our way through the hours.

Meanwhile, at home, Alex and I prepared to move me and my family to his flat in Gosforth, where at last Cathleen could have her own small bedroom. The boys shared the one at the back while Alex and I had the large front one.

The reason we had chosen the beginning of August for our wedding and our move was to co-coincide with the long summer school holidays, as Cathleen would have to change schools. Additionally, Christopher, at 16, had now left school but without any qualifications as he had no desire to continue with his schooling. We had talked long and hard about what his future should be, recognising that, with his learning difficulties, an academic career was not going to be possible. It was suggested that he might like to train as a chef and he was not averse to the idea. So I made an appointment for an interview at Northumbria College where such courses were run.

The man who interviewed us could have talked for England. It was impossible to get a word in edgeways but the burden of his discourse was to sing the praises of a catering course where baking and confectionery were taught and which would begin the following month. Our attempts to bring the conversation back to a course on cookery was swept aside in the torrent of praise for the course of his choice, and as the minutes, and then the hours, passed it would be no exaggeration to say that we were browbeaten into signing Chris up for the two-year catering course. Much later we staggered out of the building to find a concerned Alex who had been wondering whether we had sneaked out and left by the back door! But the deed was done and Chris was signed up to learn all about his new career.

We went to see several of the local schools to find one

to suit Cathleen. It would have to be one with as small a class as possible as we were aware that she would need more help than she would find in a larger class, so we chose the local Church School situated on Gosforth High Street. However, within a short time of her going there, it was evident that she needed more care than the school could provide. We therefore requested that she be given a place in a special school and we made an appointment to go and see the headmistress of a newly built one near Cramlington. We were most impressed by the high standard of the school where the children were taught such things as how to go shopping and other practical aspects of life. Many of the children were from underprivileged families but there was a great atmosphere between the staff and the children.

The headmistress told us of an occasion when some of the children had been taken for a visit to the seaside, not more than 9 or 10 miles away. It became obvious that for one little boy this was his first visit to the coast as, stepping out of the school combi at the seafront, he gaped in astonishment at the sea, turned to the teacher and in a broad Geordie accent asked, 'Ee missus, whee put aal that waatter there?'

She was somewhat bemused that we had instigated the request for Cathleen to attend, as mostly placements were made against a lot of resistance from the parents, but we knew that Cathleen would need the specialised education that the school could provide.

When he had asked me to marry him, Alex had asked me if I would like to give up work. While I appreciated his thoughtfulness, I did not feel that I would want to stay at home and become a housewife, but was keen to further my career. To that end, I signed up for a fresh Civil Service course starting in September, this one being aimed at those who would take the exam leading to promotion to Executive Officer. The course was to be held in the same gloomy building as the previous one, but this time there were not so many people who had signed up for it, and although one or two did drop out at least there were enough desks for all of us from the start. The subjects were mathematics, general knowledge and English language, and this time although the building was as cold and cheerless as before, at least I was ferried there and back by my husband.

Moving in with Alex meant that the flat on Chillingham Road was now vacant. I would have preferred to have sold it but house prices were static at that time and, with no profit to be made, solicitor and estate agent fees would be heavy. I made a few attempts to advertise it but only succeeded in attracting a lady who was looking for somewhere at a knock-down price, so reluctantly we decided to rent it furnished.

Strict rules were still in place regarding the rights of tenants in a rented flat if it was let unfurnished, but if it was furnished then it was possible to agree a contract for six months or a year and to regain occupation should the rent not be paid. So we juggled the furniture in both our flats, keeping the pieces we valued and putting the rest into my old flat. At that point, Alex's daughter Jacqueline visited us one evening and asked if her current boyfriend could have the flat as he was having to leave the one he was in. It was of course up to me, and neither of us had ever met this young man, but as it was Alex's daughter who was asking, I agreed and we rented it out at a reasonable rate which would cover the mortgage repayments. Alex's downstairs flat was let furnished to a couple of young girls and helped him to pay the mortgage on his. We seldom saw them and it worked well.

I was able to walk to work again, in fact the journey was somewhat shorter than before and we soon settled into our new routine. There was no space for a washing machine in the flat and so once a week we would collect all the laundry, load it into the car and take it to the nearby launderette where we would sit comfortably and enjoy a Mars Bar each as our weekly treat.

Changes were taking place as legislation had been brought in to provide a smoke-free atmosphere; smoke-encrusted buildings were being cleaned and while central heating for all was still a long way off, we now had to buy smoke-free fuel for the fireplace which heated the flat and the water. Alex also had a go at making some beer, but this was less than successful when the jars exploded and left the airing cupboard with a ripe yeasty smell!

Meanwhile Paul had decided that he was no longer interested in training as a quantity surveyor. While I was disappointed, as I knew how important it was for him to have some sort of a career, there was little I could do to persuade him. He left and applied for a job at Long Benton, the central office where I worked. While not ideal, it would be possible for him to succeed if he found the work to his liking, but I had my doubts.

The Central Office of the Ministry of Health and Social Security, was a place where one worked, had a relative working there or knew of someone who worked there. Staff were bussed in from as far away as Consett in County Durham, so it was not unusual when someone learned where you worked to be asked, 'Oh, do you know so-and-so?' Generally the answer was no, although on one occasion it did happen to be the girl working opposite me! So it was not surprising that Paul should look for a job there.

We bought a corgi from Auntie Maryon. She gave us a special price for him providing we would let him be used for breeding purposes. We called him Teddy and he had a nasty habit of nipping any passing ankle.

At about the same time there was an unexpected visit to England of my aunt, Gladys, who had gone to Australia and was married there in the 1930s. Gladys was the youngest of my paternal grandparents' six children and had been somewhat spoiled. She had met her future husband at a country dance near Keswick when holidaying there with her sister and some friends. Isaac came from a family who had a farm on the far slopes of Skiddaw near Bassenthwaite and was already in the process of arranging to emigrate to Australia when he met Gladys. On his way to start his journey he called upon my grandfather to ask for her hand in marriage, and some time later grandfather paid for her passage to go and be married out there. They had run a fruit farm on the Murray River near Mildura and during the war often sent us parcels of raisins and sultanas. Before she died, her sister, my Aunt Ethel and my guardian, had gone over there and stayed for a year. Now Gladys was to come and visit her remaining sister Maryon and their brother Harry – my father, his brother Stan and Ethel all having died in the intervening years. With her was her only child, my cousin Peter.

Gladys had visited England once just before the outbreak of war when Peter had been five years old, and I had vague recollections of that time. They had left from Tilbury and I recalled their ship pulling away from the dock with Peter's red cap being waved as they gradually set out into the Thames. Now we were to meet again.

Peter, now in his late thirties was a handsome, well set-up man while Gladys had turned into a slightly large and breathless elderly lady, unlike her older sister who was whippet thin. It appeared that she also had some heart problems, but instead of being housed in comfort in Uncle Harry's centrally heated modern home, she was to stay at Woodburn. At that point, Maryon had yet to reduce it to her normal state of disintegration, having only recently moved in after inheriting it from Ethel, but none the less, it was still a draughty and comfortless house for a lady used to a warmer climate.

Uncle Harry and his wife did their bit by picking up the two visitors most days and taking them out for various trips around the countryside, much to Maryon's annoyance as she was not included. It seemed that when the siblings got together fierce verbal arguments would break out, much like the ones

I had had to endure as a teenager when Maryon had lived in Woodburn with Ethel, my father and me. I was pleased that I was not around to witness these altercations which, it appeared, had a lot to do with who had been left what in various wills. Perhaps that was the underlying reason for the visit.

Peter was handsome and amiable, but before long he would excuse himself in the evenings and disappear, not to return until the early hours of the morning. With no sign of a wife or girlfriend in the offing, it seemed to us that he might very well have been 'batting for the other side', as the saying goes. Certainly he seemed to earn a very good living as a model back home, not that that meant a great deal. I couldn't help wondering how Gladys felt about her son. They seemed to get on very well so perhaps she was glad not to have to face the prospect of a daughter-in-law.

They came to have a meal with us in our cramped little flat, but I was a bit worried about the heavy cold that Gladys had. It was winter, as they had probably chosen this time to travel when air fares would be cheaper, but I was concerned that it might not have been a wise choice. A few days later we learned that Gladys was confined to bed, so I went down to see her that night. I didn't like the look of her, taking into consideration her heart problems, so I took Peter to one side, saying that while I didn't want to worry him unduly, I felt that the doctor should be called as she should probably be taken to hospital. The next day she was admitted to the Royal Victoria Infirmary, better known as the RVI, and a few days later she died of pneumonia and heart failure.

There was no question of Uncle Isaac coming to the UK, so the funeral was held in the nearest available crematorium in North Shields as the local facilities were under pressure due to illnesses and deaths at that time of the year. Peter returned alone to Australia and we gradually lost touch with him afterwards.

91

A couple of weeks later, Alex had taken Teddy out for a walk when the dog suddenly darted across the street into the path of a car and was killed. We hadn't had him for long but we were all saddened by his death. Alex and I took him out into the country at night and found a quiet spot to bury him and Maryon said she might have another dog for us before long.

Most evenings Alex was able to pick me up outside work, and once Paul started working there we would wait for him too. But one night, just as he was about to get into the car, he excused himself and said he would see us later. Somewhat bemused we watched as he walked over to a girl with a dog on a lead and began to talk to her. We drove off and it was much later before he returned home.

Her name was Clara and she was a Spanish girl working in England as an au pair. Apparently one of Paul's friends worked as a draughtsman in the offices of a shipyard on the Tyne where a Chilean ship had put in for a long-term refit. The Chilean sailors were attending an English course for foreigners at the local college where Clara was also going to learn English. So when the Chilean sailors decided to throw a party, they invited the staff at the shipyard plus Clara and others in the language class, and Paul went along and met her there. He explained all this when he came home, and it seemed that he must have made an impression because she had walked all the way to the Ministry on the offchance of seeing him, although the house where she was living and working was some distance away. However, he said he was not too keen on her as she was older than him, 25 to his 20.

Although it was winter, unless there was the possibility of snow we still spent most weekends at the cottage, taking Cathleen with us and leaving the boys to have the flat to themselves and their friends. Clara apparently became a frequent visitor and began to lend Paul large illustrated books on Spain, the wonders of Madrid and the gleaming coastlines. Never having really settled in England with its dismal climate compared with the warmth of South Africa, Paul was obviously beguiled. Before long, and not to my surprise, he had decided that work at the Ministry was not for him, and he answered an advert and obtained a job with the car hire firm Avis which, being car mad, was more to his taste.

That spring, one of the girls at work organised a day trip to Holland to see the bulb fields, and Alex and I decided to go. Flying on a rather ancient plane, we took off from Newcastle Airport and after a turbulent journey through thick cloud we were met by a bus at the other end. The weather perked up and we had a wonderful day touring the colourful fields, visiting the pottery factory and having a splendid lunch at a seaside hotel. We then went to Kierkenhof Gardens and enjoyed strolling under the trees beside the brilliant flowerbeds. On the way back to the airport we drove through The Hague and caught a glimpse of the canals and their bridges. The flight back was calmer than the one out and we returned home tired, but with wonderful memories of a beautiful country.

It was marvellous to be able to do things like that as a couple and we both took a great deal of pleasure in planning and arranging our lives. At last I was enjoying a relationship with a man whom I could trust, who had the same outlook on life as I did and who was willing to have us work together on every aspect of our lives. There were no undercurrents, no sulks, no unexplained absences, only a day-to-day agreement over the smallest details of our lives. At times it was hard not to make comparisons, but better in the long run to look ahead and concentrate on the future.

8

At work it was taking me some time to get used to my new surname. At times I felt as if I was living in a land of aliases. First of all born Trobe, then Malone and now Lowther, although I liked my new surname. I remembered when Anne was born, Aunt Nancy, my cousin Bill's mother, asked me what we were going to call the new baby. When I told her she was to be called Anne, Nancy said, 'What a good name! After all, Malone isn't a very nice name, is it?' As she had recently remarried – having been a widow for some years after the death of her husband Stan, my father's younger brother – and was now called Cook, there really wasn't anything to say to that.

At work as we trawled day by day through the records of the children of the whole country, from time to time strange surnames would be brought to our attention and we often wondered at their origins. But closer to home was the subject of Cathleen's surname and after talking it over we decided that in her own interests, it would be best for her name to be changed to Lowther as well. So we made an appointment with our solicitor and at the same time had our wills drawn up. I had never bothered with a will before as I had very little of this world's goods, but Alex felt we should do so now, and I agreed. The wills were quite simple. Everything was left to each other and on the deaths of both of us the five children, my four and Alex's one, would inherit whatever we owned by then. The changing of Cathleen's name was quite simple as well. As I was a widow all that was needed was a signed statement by me that I wished her name to be changed. Copies of this document then went to her school and onto her medical records and that was that, so in the future she would not have to give involved explanations as to why her name was different from that of her parents.

One of the girls working on our section was married to a miner, and once more the country was in the grip of strikes by miners, and by many other firms as well. The three-day week was imposed and often there would be electricity cuts without any warning. Edward Heath decided to go to the country in order to resolve the matter and was resoundingly defeated in the ensuing election. England became known as 'the sick man of Europe' and it was a most stressful time. However it was then, with our next pay round and my incremental increase, that I first earned £100 per month. I was told that a few years previously Harold Wilson had said that his ambition for the working classes was for everyone to earn such a monthly sum, and at last I had. Unfortunately it did not seem to improve our finances to any great degree.

From time to time I would receive a nice long letter from Anne. She was working in the evenings and weekends at an upmarket bar in central Croydon and was still seeing Dave. One of the regulars at the bar fancied himself as a bit of a poet and she sent me reams of his poetry which was obviously making a deep impression. Whether or not this sent a warning shot across the bows on Dave's part, the next bit of news was that they were engaged and would be marrying on April 1st of that year, 1972. Meanwhile they both worked as hard as they could to raise enough money for a deposit on a house. It wasn't going to be easy to raise a mortgage, as Dave had recently started up his own business as a driving instructor and as a self-employed man did not have enough years as yet of proven profit-and-loss accounts. However, they were able to overcome this and bought an old house on the outskirts of Croydon in the suburb of Norbury.

95

We all went down for the wedding and Cathleen as a flower girl was the only bridesmaid. It would have been difficult to pick anyone else as, although Dave came from a large family, they were all boys except the eldest, Sheila, who was quite a lot older than Anne, and the youngest whom she didn't know very well. Anne's new surname was to be Shirley. Surprisingly she had a new sister-in-law whose first name was also Shirley, making her Shirley Shirley. They had moved into their new home and Dave was busy working on it to bring it up to a better standard.

The wedding took place in a local church, where Alex gave Anne away, and the reception was held in a restaurant situated in the woods outside Croydon. Our party was a bit outnumbered by Dave's relatives but it was a happy occasion and everyone cheered them off as they left in their car for their honeymoon.

Back in Newcastle things were not looking very good for Alex, as the firm he worked for, Armour, were about to close down all their operations and he would soon be out of a job. It was hard to decide whether to look for a new job now, or to hang on for as long as it was likely to take in order to take advantage of his redundancy package. In the event he decided to hang on and we were able to buy a car, a two-year-old cream Ford Capri, with the redundancy proceeds to replace the one he had had from the firm.

Finding a new job was not easy as unemployment was high at that time, but he finally took one as an insurance salesman doing door-to-door selling. Meanwhile I continued with my evening classes for the EO exam and also did some research on the possibility of taking an Open University course. I obtained all the literature and I was quite impressed with the idea of working at it module by module. The only drawback was that many of the accompanying lectures were done on BBC 2 on the television and we did not have a set that received that channel, so of necessity that had to be put on hold.

TV was still mainly watched in black and white, and at that time the format in which it was broadcast was to be changed. Eventually we would have had to buy a new set, but at that point we did not have the finances to do so. But it did not really matter as we spent every weekend up at the cottage and evenings were filled with my classes or with sitting in the launderette doing the family wash.

We heard from Auntie Maryon that she had a dog she thought we would like, so we hurried over to Woodburn that evening. As we walked into her living room we were confronted by an almost-grown corgi with an alert expression who pranced up to us with, I would swear it, a big smile on his face. Cathleen took one look at him and knelt down on the floor to gather him up into her arms, where he enthusiastically licked her face. We stood there with big grins on our faces as the two of them romped around the floor. We decided to call him Bobby and we took him home with us that night.

The following weekend we took him up to the cottage with us, where he and Cathleen were to spend many happy times wandering around the hills and along the valley above the cottage. The deal was that when he was fully grown, from time to time Maryon would have him back to service one of her bitches, so for most of his adult life he would go off for his 'holiday' and became the father of several litters of pups.

From time to time we would be invited to afternoon tea on a Sunday with Alex's mother. She was a splendid pastry cook and Cathleen loved these visits, and would make a point of sampling each of the cakes and pies on offer. It was lovely for her to have grandparents at last and Annie was a wonderful woman who took a great interest in the child. She kept their bungalow absolutely spotless while Ossie worked hard on their garden producing a wealth of fruit and vegetables. Once a week they would meet up with Ossie's family for coffee on the High Street and every year went for a holiday, mostly to a large hotel in Scarborough where they enjoyed the visiting orchestra. Ossie was a violinist and in his heyday had played in an orchestra himself.

The transposing of the Family Allowance details onto the computer was fast coming to an end and everyone was wondering where we were likely to be sent. It must have been quite a headache to fit everyone back into suitable places and while the majority would no doubt be returning to Family Allowances, there was some envy when I was given my new posting which proved to be to Personnel. For some reason this was felt to be the top end of the employment tree. I was given the number of the room to which I would report on the Monday after our section was broken up.

It proved to be the section that dealt with the pay records for the staff in the whole of the country, and the HEO in charge of it turned out to be a Salvationist whom I knew, the bandmaster at the City Temple Corps. I was introduced into the section where I would be working and initially went to sit with a man called Charles, who was to show me the ropes. Charles was a widower with three daughters who had initially come from London but was now happily living in this far-off outpost of the country.

This section was dealing with the weekly pay records and each week we would receive reams of computer printouts which had to be scanned for errors and corrected. We also dealt with new entrants and leavers, and saw to their P45s and checked their tax records.

I no longer walked to work with Agnes of course, once I had moved, but we met up from time to time. She had returned to work at Family Allowances where it seemed chaos reigned. On the numerous occasions since then, when I have heard that some section or other of government business is to be computerised, I have happily sat back and waited for the inevitable confusion and backlog that always seems to ensue.

This was the first very large section to be so reconstructed. Previously things had trundled along quite calmly with a final section of people who had the task of preparing and printing the order books before they were sent out to the mothers. Now this section was to be disbanded and other work found for them, but many of them were not capable of more complicated tasks and there were several distressing breakdowns and early retirements.

The IT specialists who had set up the scheme had not allowed for the length of time it would take for a computer printout to arrive at the desk of the CO dealing with a new claim before it could be awarded. Consequently, before long there was a six-month backlog of first claims and the staff were feeling the pressure of dealing with the new system. I was quite glad, therefore, to be working on a different type of task and, although I didn't appreciate it at the time, the experience of working with a payroll would stand me in good stead in the future.

Soon the night-school course came to an end and I made my application to take the next EO examination. It was held in a large room in a building in town with rows and rows of desks as we worked through the various papers. I felt quite confident and enjoyed writing the essays and tackling the maths. The only problem was that smoking was allowed, and as it was a cold day all the windows were closed. Gradually the smoke gathered up in the ceiling and descended into a choking cloud all around us. I struggled to complete the final maths paper and eventually was glad to escape out into the fresh air where Alex was waiting for me. However, when I got my results I had done quite well, only losing a few marks out of a possible 400.

The next hurdle was to be an interview and prior to it, an IQ test. Never having been all that good at puzzles, I took the precaution of buying a little paperback book called 'Test your own IQ' which proved to be invaluable, as on the day I sailed through the test without any trouble. There wasn't a long wait after taking the IQ test so I suppose it was quickly marked so that the board members had the results in front of them. I found the interview most enjoyable. The questions they asked me ranged far and wide, and once more they were interested in my time in South Africa and also asked me a lot about the renovation of the cottage. I came out feeling I had done my best and settled back into work to wait and see if I would be offered a post.

One night Jacqueline called in to the flat in some distress. She and her boyfriend had broken up as he had met someone else, and he had moved out of the flat on Chillingham Road. We gave what comfort we could. She spent the evening with us and the next night we took the keys and went down to the flat. The young man had obviously spent many hours busily painting an enormous American Stars and Stripes flag on one wall of the large front room and a smaller version of the Union Jack on the back of the door! Both were going to take some covering but mainly what we were considering was the possibility of having the two flats renovated by bringing the outside toilets inside. Generous grants were on offer for the work to be done, but consequently the market was overheated and it was not easy to find three builders who would provide the necessary quotes. However, we decided to go ahead.

Before doing so I went to see Mrs Robson, my tenant in the upstairs flat. She was an elderly widow who paid a very low controlled rent which had been collected by an agency when I first bought the flats. The agency was sold on to another company who found the accounts in some sort of chaos, and certainly I had never received any money from them as there always seemed to have been repairs to do as well as their charges to cover. The new company sent me a cheque for £50 and almost before I could deposit it, asked for it back as they said they had made a mistake. Rather stupidly I suppose, I sent it back, but at the same time dispensed with their services and provided Mrs Robson with a paying-in book for her to deposit her rent at the branch of my local bank just up the road.

I explained to her that I was considering upgrading her flat as well as the one downstairs and she was quite keen on the idea. The council were also offering tenants such as herself the chance to move into alternative accommodation while the work took place, but when I mentioned this to her, Mrs Robson went into a great huff, accusing me of trying to evict her from her home. I managed to calm her down but from then on she viewed anything with suspicion. Nevertheless I got the requisite quotes and selected a builder and before long the work commenced.

Newcastle and its surroundings were in the process of changing in many ways. A tunnel was being built under the Tyne, further down the river; a motorway was built on the Newcastle side of the Tyne bridge, slicing through what had been the bottleneck of the town; and in the town centre large swathes of old buildings were demolished to make way for a huge shopping centre behind the main streets. Unfortunately, some lovely Georgian buildings disappeared in this sweeping change and there was much annoyance in many quarters.

A road was planned to link up with the road to the coast from the Haymarket and along Jesmond Road towards Armstrong Bridge and the valley in which Woodburn stood. Models of the new development were on show at the church hall at the top of Benton Bank. But none of that came to pass, as groups of people banded together to protest and to demand an enquiry. By the time that had been looked into, there was no money for the project anyway.

To the north of Newcastle most of the mines had been closed and large opencast mining was taking place. Once all the coal had been collected the areas were beautifully landscaped and excellent road systems put in place. Soon new towns were springing up and much light industry was brought in to give new employment to the area.

In Byker, the area where my maternal grandmother had brought up her family in the early years of the century, many of the old streets were demolished and the families re-housed in new council housing north of the city. In their place rose a building containing flats but imaginatively constructed in many curves and with wide walkways outside the flats. Before long it had been re-christened as 'The Wall'.

Many other changes were taking place, the most important at that time being the legislation to provide smoke-free air. Many older people had died over previous years because of the terrible smogs, especially in the larger cities, where those with heart or lung diseases had succumbed to the choking fumes from industrial and house chimneys. Now everyone had to buy smoke-free fuel for their fires instead of coal and gradually the winter skies were clearing. In addition North Sea gas was now available and teams of workers were building pipelines across the country to supply the towns and cities. As I walked to work, the huge gasometer at the foot of the hill gradually fell into disuse, as we were all converted to the new gas, and large buildings began to be cleaned of their years of grime.

Christopher was doing well on his catering course and most weeks he would bring home a fresh type of bread, many of which I had never seen before. There were cottage loaves, loaves packed with fruit, loaves with marzipan inside and many more, and we eagerly looked forward to each week's baking. It hardly mattered that it did my weight no favours!

Paul was still seeing Clara and her tales of the splendours of Spain seemed to be making a big impression on him. With the family starting to strike out into adulthood, it was obvious that many changes would take place over the next few years. Initially, of course, there would be whatever posting might come my way as an EO. Strictly speaking it could be anywhere in the country and at that time there were many vacancies in the London area, but people from the north were reluctant to go, as the house prices were so much higher.

To try and solve the difficulties, the government had moved some of the work to other areas, for instance the National Savings section was now based in Durham and War Pensions in Blackpool. Other than such larger organisations, there were posts in many of the local offices up and down the country, or even a post in Central Office itself. There was no way of telling but we both felt that change was in the air, and that summer we would often drive out into the Northumberland countryside or spend time looking at various housing developments, as whatever happened we intended to move to a larger house.

For the first summer we had decided to let the cottage as a holiday home and I had put an advert in the magazine circulated at Central Office, as I could deal with any enquiries on site. The money helped to pay the loan we had been given by the council. Unable therefore to use it ourselves, we made good use of our weekends by driving far and wide.

Anne and Dave came north for a holiday and we took a week off as well, introducing them to the Northumberland coast with trips to Lindisfarne, Alnwick, Hexham and Durham. Quite an eye-opener for Dave I expect, as he was under the impression that we lived among coalfields and shipyards, many of which were now long gone.

Alex suggested that we should go and see the crystal ball man again and arranged a meeting at his home. Shortly after we met, Alex had told me that he too had had readings from him while he was still on his own and that he had been told he would meet someone from overseas who had a uniform hanging behind the door. The crystal ball man had also said he could see a cottage with a stream running beside it, all

103

of which had come true. He looked much as I remembered him as we sat in his kitchen and he produced the ball from its velvet wrapping. Alex went first and was told that he could see large sums of money, cheques, coming his way but also that he would move and it would be across the water, which could have meant anything.

Then it was my turn and the crystal ball man became very solemn. He said he could see someone close to me and he was suffering a lot of pain. He gestured to his chest. It was close to a public holiday, he continued, but he was always there watching over me. I felt quite faint as Ron, my first husband, had indeed died of coronary thrombosis, in great pain, and it had been the day after a South African public holiday.

Somewhat shaken, we left and I decided that I would not seek to see what the future might hold again. It was almost four years since I had arrived back in England with my four children. Taking stock, much had happened after the early struggles and my unhappy run-in with Louie. The future now looked to be opening up for the children: Anne was happily married, Paul had a good job and Christopher had trained for a worthwhile career. Cathleen meanwhile was now attending a school which could give her the extra help that she needed. For myself, I now had a husband I loved and could trust and we had proved during our first year together that we were able to work in harness with the same aims and standards. Now we waited to see what the next move would be when my posting came through.

9

One day the HEO Mr P. called me into his office and, inviting me to sit down, told me that I had been offered a post as EO at Sunderland South Local Office. At Central Office our dealings were with the country as a whole and we rarely, if ever, came into contact with the public. At the local office level, however, there would be a constant stream of people passing through the doors and the work was divided into two distinct departments: benefits paid out on the basis of contributions made by employees, and benefits which were based upon need. The latter, non-contributory benefits, were known at that time as Supplementary Benefits and could be given in addition to Contributory Benefits where there was a need, or in cases where contributions were deficient.

Contributory Benefits were based strictly on the amount of payments the applicant had made into the system and at that time these took the form of a weekly 'stamp'. Smaller firms would still physically buy the stamps and place them on cards, deduct the amount from the wages, and at the end of the year send the cards to Records in Central Office to be counted and recorded. Larger firms dispensed with the stamping system and made payments in bulk. Although there were 52 weeks in the year, 50 weeks would be considered as a full record. I was to be an Executive Officer on the Contributory Benefits side where the payments being made were for sickness and invalidity benefits, injury and industrial benefit, and where pension claims were checked and awarded.

Sunderland South Local Office was situated in the centre of the town, but over on the other side of the River Wear was its sister office, Sunderland North. As I was one of two EOs newly appointed to the area, the other lady was to work at Sunderland North, but it had been decided that for training purposes we would swop over and she would train at Sunderland South and I would train at Sunderland North.

I had been informed that a move out of the area might qualify me for various expenses, so I made enquiries, but it seemed that Sunderland was classed as a local appointment and I would only be entitled to the difference in travelling expenses for a period of five years. Nonetheless it was still our intention to move and so we set about exploring the area.

Although the town was not all that far away from Newcastle, it was one I had never visited. It was further south and closer to the coast so that it was some way off the north/south highway. The town itself was a good size; situated on the River Wear it was still a shipbuilding town, the main shipbuilders specialising in smaller working ships at a time when many shipyards had closed down. One or two local coal mines still existed but there was a lot of unemployment and the local unemployment office were kept very busy indeed. Unlike north of the Tyne, Sunderland had not benefited from new light industry or good road networks at that point.

There was a good shopping centre and a market hall, as well as a large departmental store called Binns. Council housing abounded and it was necessary to move further out of town to find any private housing estates, but we toured the areas every weekend to see where we might be able to buy a house.

The first house we looked at was a dormer bungalow with small bedrooms upstairs while downstairs the rooms were tiny and somewhat claustrophobic. The next one turned out to be on a very new estate with rows of houses lined up on a hillside and swarming with small children. Another was quite nice but all the front gardens were open plan, which

I did not care for. At the next one we did not even get out of the car as it was set right next to a pub. The hunt went on and meanwhile I caught the local train from Gosforth into Newcastle Central Station every day and changed there for the train to Sunderland.

News had come from Anne that she and Dave were expecting their first child in October and so I got out the knitting needles. As I travelled on the train I used the time to knit a complicated pattern into a christening robe, or whatever Anne wanted to use it for. I was thrilled to be becoming a grandmother at such an early age, but sad that she was living so far away.

We still went up to the cottage as often as possible. During the first summer after its completion we had rented it out as a holiday cottage, but we found that it wasn't worthwhile as at the end of the season we had to redecorate the whole place and the electric cooker had to be replaced after sundry spills had been left unattended, putting several of the plates out of action.

Paul was still seeing Clara and her parents came over to England for a visit. We took them up to the cottage for the afternoon but relations were strained as they spoke no English and we spoke no Spanish. Clara soon got fed up with trying to translate for us all and the company fell into two camps, Clara and her parents and Paul and his. Soon it would be time for her to return to Spain as her visa ran out.

Meanwhile we continued house hunting in Sunderland. Eventually we found a house on the western side of town, on a recently built estate. It was semi-detached, situated at the end of a cul-de-sac with a small front garden and an enormous back one where the owner had done absolutely nothing, leaving us a blank canvas. In truth the last thing I had ever wanted was a semi in the suburbs, but there was very little choice in our price range. Prices were beginning to move upwards somewhat and we were lucky to secure it at £11,000. At that time it was usual to pay 10 per cent as a deposit and borrow the rest, so Alex went to his building society, the Nationwide, to ask for a mortgage. He was turned down as they said that at that point they had run out of funds and would not be lending any money for another three months. So I made an appointment and went to see my father's friend Archie Morrison, who was the manager of the Newcastle Building Society where I had my mortgage for the flats at Chillingham Road. I had had no trouble in arranging that loan. However, still not being totally au fait with the vagaries of the British tax system, it came as a bit of a shock when Archie approached me in some embarrassment to say that I was not entitled to have two mortgages, as tax relief could only be given on one. We solved it by getting an offer of £3,000 for Alex's flats, paying off the remaining £1,500 on mine at Chillingham Road and putting £1,000 as a deposit and using the rest for the solicitor's costs.

When we moved in, however, we discovered that the sellers had stripped the house of every hook, towel and curtain rail. If it had been screwed on, they had taken it! Nevertheless, we liked the house, it had gas central heating, a new experience for us and had a pleasant outlook. It was also more spacious than our flat, which we had sold without a backward glance.

Alex's mum Annie and his stepfather Ossie, came down to visit us as soon as we had settled in, but not long afterwards we received bad news. Annie was diagnosed with rectal cancer and was admitted to the Royal Victoria Infirmary for a colostomy. When we went to visit her she was as bright and courageous as ever, and said the surgeon had assured her that 'they had got it all out'. She went on to have chemotherapy and made a good recovery, but I knew how difficult it must have been for that dainty and fastidious woman to have to cope with a colostomy bag.

Clara had returned to Spain and Paul had gone down to see her off on the ship to Santander which was not too far from her home in northern Spain. On hearing that we had moved to Sunderland, Avis offered him the post of manager at the new office they were setting up there, but he turned it down and we discovered what his plans were. Clara was going to go and live in Majorca, where her uncle and aunt lived, and Paul was going to go and live there too. I was not happy but managed to conceal my feelings as I knew he had never really settled in England. He stayed with us in Sunderland for a week or two but then we took him to Newcastle Airport to catch his flight. He had booked a package holiday and planned to stay on after he had spent his two weeks in his hotel. I put a brave face on as we waved him off, but on our return home I unexpectedly dissolved into tears. He was 21, able to make his own decisions, and had set his sights on a different way of life.

The years that followed would not always be easy for him. Spanish authorities did not take kindly to non-Spaniards taking jobs in the travel industry, but initially he was able to get a job with Avis in Majorca based at an hotel near Magaluf. The other man at this office was Spanish and between him and Clara Paul began to learn the language. Eventually he would get a work permit and become involved at the airport, working for Dan Air when they were at their height.

Christopher spent a short time with us but deciding he preferred Newcastle to Sunderland, he returned there and lived at the flat in Chillingham Road for a few weeks before the builders moved in. Then he took a room in a house in Gosforth, mostly filled with students at the local Teachers Training College where he met Maggie. She haled from Doncaster, and was coming towards the end of her training as a teacher. Her mother was a widow and she had two elder brothers. Before long we met her and liked her very much.

So suddenly the home that had been teeming with the boys and their friends was eerily silent. When doing my grocery shopping I still found myself catering for large numbers and it took me some time to come to grips with the fact that there were only three of us. It all seemed to have happened so quickly.

Before long we were invited over for the evening by our nextdoor neighbours, Ted and Betty Leach. They were much the same age group as ourselves with one son who was just about to go to university. We had an enjoyable time finding that we had much in common. Apparently Ted used to work for the same insurance company that Alex was working for and was not surprised that Alex was not too happy with them. He himself had left them and was a manager of a large carpet store. Betty worked part-time in the corsetry department of Binns. Before long we went out regularly to our local for an evening's chat, enjoying each other's company.

One day we went on a trip to Barnard Castle and spent the afternoon wandering around the pleasant little town and looking in the shops. We went into one where the atmosphere was redolent of spices and which held a large array of small gifts and items which could be used to beautify a home. Betty however, knew exactly what she was looking for but did not know quite how to describe it until, to the delight of the rest of us, she collared a salesperson saying, 'Have you got any of those smelly balls?'

Of course she meant the carved wooden balls impregnated with various spicy scents, but ever since, when occasionally buying the same thing myself, I have to smile in memory of that day.

Alex went for an interview for a job with the gas company where they sent him for a medical and he was found to be suffering from diabetes. He went to his GP who told him that he must return to the weight he had been as a young man. He was not particularly overweight, but it certainly didn't do him any harm to lose a few pounds. With his usual determination he put himself on a strict diet, two boiled eggs

110

in the morning, two apples for lunch and a salad made of chopped cabbage with tomato at night, with an occasional steak at the weekend. After a couple of months he had lost his excess weight and was no longer testing positive for sugar. In those days, however, there were no regular follow-up clinics for the condition.

In the event he did not take the job with the Gas Board but opted instead to be an area Pools Organiser, covering the South Tyne area and across as far west as Consett. Local collectors took the money and the coupons to the district organiser from whom Alex collected them, the whole lot being taken to Newcastle for checking and forwarding on to the Pools company. During the week it was his job to recruit new collectors; it was all very big business in the days before the Lottery, and could be very hard work when things went wrong and people fell down on the job.

Our move meant a change for Cathleen as well and she had to leave the lovely little school she had gone to in Cramlington. The school in Sunderland was larger and did not have the same intimate feeling, in fact I was never very happy with it or with the staff there, but there was no alternative as she found it very difficult to learn. As we drove up to the cottage at the weekends we would say her numbers with her but it took a lot of effort on her part to learn to count up to 20. She loved to sing songs though and we would go through all her favourites such as 'How Much is That Doggy in the Window?' and 'Old Macdonald had a Farm' as we swept up the Wear Valley, past the big wheel at Stanhope and finally over the breast of the hill and down into Nenthead. This was her paradise where, whatever the weather, she ranged far and wide over the hills and up the valley with Bobby in close pursuit. Her favourite activity was to help Alan collect the eggs in the large huts where the hens were kept.

As part of my training I had been sent to the large training establishment at Blackpool. I caught the Carlisle train from Newcastle, changing to the Glasgow/London express as far as Preston where I changed again for the Blackpool train. Arriving at Blackpool station with the address of the B&B I was to stay at clutched firmly in my hand, I found a taxi and was driven up the north shore just beyond Bispham. The B&B was right on the seafront and run by two energetic ladies. The rooms were lovely and the food fantastic, and I soon settled in with the other girls who were also on the course. We were to spend three weeks on our training with a further week to follow after a month or two. Most of the girls came from Yorkshire, and I was not only the only one from the north-east but also the only EO. At first I got the impression they were a bit in awe of me, but we soon put that right when I explained that I had only recently reached such elevated heights myself.

On our first morning, as one woman we all declined the cooked breakfast and confined ourselves to toast and coffee. However, we soon found that by mid-morning we were famished and by lunchtime could have eaten a horse. It made more economic sense, therefore, to stoke up with a good breakfast and take a small lunch at the canteen as our breakfasts were all in, but we had to pay for our lunches!

They were a good crowd and one night we all went to see Danny La Rue at one of the theatres. What a wonderful performance it was. We were enraptured not only by his performance, but also by the magnificent gowns that he wore. We discovered that there would be a 'dress rehearsal' of the famous Blackpool lights, so that night we took the tram along the front and 'oohed' and 'aahed' at all the splendid set pieces.

During the day the training was intense. All the benefits were paid strictly according to the rules and, as the workload would be heavy, it would be necessary to have it all at our fingertips. Most claims would be straightforward with people only being off sick for a few days or at the most a couple of weeks with perhaps flu or a bad cold. It became more complicated with longer periods of illness and with the ubiquitous system of linking periods of claims that fell within a certain timescale. All the periods of sickness were recorded on a Benefit History Sheet (or BHS) where they were linked up, and accumulated whatever the illness had been. Thus, over a period, many small claims for bad backs or colds could be added up until the total of days of sickness reached the point at which it automatically became known as Invalidity Benefit which was paid at a higher rate.

All the complex rules and regulations were kept in loose-leafed books called Codes. They needed to be loose-leafed because, when back at the office, hardly a week would go by without some amendment or other being made, which had to be put into the book and recorded.

Contributory Benefits were on the second floor at Sunderland South and consisted of three sections each dealing with sickness, invalidity and injury benefit. They were divided up alphabetically with one CA to do the filing, six COs to assess the benefits, and an EO at the head of each section, whose job it was to check 10 per cent of the claims, giving advice on difficult cases and, if called upon, interviewing claimants that the COs had been unable to deal with. So I took my place at the head of my section and was soon finding much to keep me busy.

The post came in early every morning, and staff and EOs took turns to come in and deal with it. Each letter was cut along the top on a machine and then the sides were slit open, the letter date stamped and the envelope stapled to the letter or claim form. All the staff stood to do this and hands had to be on the table at all times. One CO sat at the end next to the EO and had any valuable items passed to him or her and recorded in the valuables book. The mail was roughly sorted into groups and taken to the various sections.

For each new claim, details of contributions had to be

obtained from Records in Newcastle before it could be assessed, the amount to be paid calculated and then the files packed into large holders and sent to the Finance section situated behind a locked door and presided over by another EO. Every evening the postman came in to pick up the mail with all the envelopes containing the giros that had been prepared that day.

The work was intensive with very little let-up. Behind the section were the banks of filing cabinets containing all the files in strict alphabetical order, and woe betide anyone who misfiled any papers. Hardly a day went by without some drama where files had been taken off by the staff on the lower floor where Supplementary Benefits held sway or where misfiling had taken place, when it was all hands to the pump to search the records. On one occasion a newly employed CA had to be taken off the job as the misfiling mounted up and chaos reigned until the culprit was found.

One day, out of the corner of my eye I thought I saw a familiar figure with a list in his hand, digging in the filing cabinets and checking the on-going work on the desks. A second glance confirmed my suspicion: it was Louie. He must have been sent down to Sunderland to fill in for some absentee, as that was what he did. I knew he had seen me by the way he hurriedly collected what he wanted and left, but we did not acknowledge each other. I took some quiet satisfaction that he was seeing me seated at the head of my section as an EO, as I knew that for many years he had been disgruntled that he had failed several promotion boards and this must have rubbed some salt into the wounds. He still kept in touch with my aunts, which annoyed me somewhat, but of course Maryon had known him since he was a boy and she enjoyed being taken out now and again. Alex and I visited her every week, spending an evening with her and taking Cathleen along with us. We could see the house gradually falling into disrepair about her.

114

After Louie had gone, someone told me that he had been sent down here after being taken off the work he used to do over on the west coast in the Whitehaven district, as he was being investigated for some fraudulent activity involving his expenses claims, it was thought. It did not really surprise me as he had always been prone to take any advantage, legal or otherwise, that came his way. Rightly or wrongly, I felt a deep satisfaction that I had achieved so much while he was obviously not having a very good time. Later things were to go even more drastically wrong for him, but I had no way of knowing that at that time.

His was not the only case around; our office had a problem which fortunately soon came to light and was dealt with. Often when the postman had collected the day's giro cheques and taken them off, there would be a handful of payments left over. Mindful of how anxious people were to receive their money, when the young CA offered to drop them into the mailbox on her way home, the finance EO gave them to her to post. Soon complaints began to come in of money not received and, after some investigations, it turned out that her boyfriend, who met her after work, suggested that she give him the letters. Then he had cashed the giros at various local post offices. Needless to say she lost her job, but I don't think she was prosecuted as she should not have been allowed to take the post in the first place.

Worse was to come when the deputy manager at another local office was found to have set up various bogus Supplementary Benefit accounts and used a disused house as an accommodation address to have payments delivered to him.

Two of the other EOs were ex-servicemen. One had lost a hand during the desert warfare near Tobruk when he was driving a tank, and would often amuse new people to his section by unscrewing his false hand and resting it on the desk. The other had a false leg and, although a well-built fellow, was able to get around quite well with the aid of a stick. When called upon to go into the interview room to settle some dispute or other, he would lumber in and before sitting down would slap his stick onto the desk with a loud crack which probably caused the complainer to lower both his voice as well as his expectations somewhat. I did not mind this aspect of the job and would find the best tactic was to sit quietly until the complainant had had their say, often at high decibels, before attempting to unravel whatever the problem was.

Up in Newcastle the work on the flats at Chillingham Road was almost completed and I sent in the forms to claim the 50 per cent grant and also to ask for a council loan for the other half. Before long a letter arrived approving the grant but refusing the loan, on the grounds that I did not live in one of the properties myself. This was a blow and at first I did not know what to do. After giving it some thought I wrote to the MP for that area setting out the facts and concluding by saying that my husband and I were working people with a minimal income and that while we had a nice home and indoor bathroom, I did not see why my tenants should be denied the same facility. Before long another letter came from the council saying they had re-examined their accounts and found that they would be able to extend me the loan for the balance after all!

I had noticed in the office that when, from time to time, a benefit enquiry came in where a claimant had written asking the MP to help, the file would come heavily flagged and at all points would be dealt with personally by the manager himself. If it worked for them, then why not for me?

Christopher had used the flat for a while, but now he and Maggie were renting a furnished flat up in Gosforth. I needed to find tenants for the downstairs flat where the family and I had lived, but it needed to be someone reliable as it would be let furnished. My aunt May had a friend whose young

116

daughter and her pal were eager to leave home and set up independently, so having met them and found them to be a nice pair of girls, I arranged for them to move in. However it was not long before two things happened. One of the girls decided to go back home for some reason, and the other one found out she was pregnant with no prospect of marriage. I went round to see her and she was resolved to have her child and to make a go of it. She wanted to have the flat redecorated, which I could not really afford, but she suggested that if I bought the materials as and when she did a room, she would tackle the decorating herself. This seemed a good idea all round and so from time to time I would receive a bundle of receipts and I would send her the money, and it worked well.

It was at this time that councils around the country were providing young girls who became pregnant with council flats while Social Security made sure they had enough to live on. In some cases, over the years, this has turned out to be a mixed blessing. Certainly no one would want to return to the times when young women often had no choice but to have their babies adopted, even though they would dearly have loved to keep them; on the other hand, this often led to immature young girls ending up caring for a demanding baby before their lives had really started. However, for my tenant it turned out well, as she was a more mature girl and coped well, while for my part I was assured of getting the rent.

In October came a tearful phone call from Anne. Her baby had arrived and labour had been harder than she had imagined it would be. The baby was to be called Claire and I went down to London for a few days to help out and to see my first grandchild. She was beautiful with big blue eyes and it was clear that her hair would be blonde. Anne and Dave had sold their first house and moved into a nice little three-bedroomed place in Thornton Heath which Dave was busy decorating in the time he had spare from his business as a driving instructor.

Back home we settled into our new house and began to do something with the back garden which was devoid of any plants, merely covered with low-quality grass. Alex, however, while not all that keen on gardening as such, loved any sort of garden architecture – paths, patios, rockeries, you name it, he would build it, so gradually things began to take shape.

10

In 1975 a phone call came from Paul to tell us that he and Clara were to be married that October. The wedding was to be held in a monastery in the hills beyond Clara's home, a village called Escalante, some miles from Santander in northern Spain, and the service was to be conducted by one of the monks who was a childhood friend of Clara. To get there we would have to fly to Bilbao where we would be met by Paul and Clara.

Arranging time off work was no problem for me, but when Alex made his request he was turned down, as it was into the height of the football season. As this was an occasion not to be missed he resigned the week before we left. Money was short and to raise sufficient he cashed in an insurance policy, while in order to buy a wedding outfit I went to a shop in Newcastle called Fine Feathers. This was not a charity shop: many of the 'county set' put clothes in for sale and received a percentage of the price while the owner kept the rest. Consequently it was possible to buy a barely worn, top-of-the-range outfit at a reasonable price, so it was here that I was able to buy a lovely dress and jacket, just right for the occasion. Never having been a lover of hats, I was happy to be told that it was not felt necessary to wear one at Spanish weddings, which was a huge relief to say nothing of the expense.

Christopher and Cathleen were to go with us but Anne, being heavily pregnant with her second child due just after Christmas, was unable to attend. Flights to Bilboa, of course, went from Heathrow, so once more it would be necessary to make our way to London first. This worked out quite well as we took Bobby with us and he was looked after by Anne while we were away. We left the car at their house and took a taxi to Croydon station before catching the train to London and the connection to Heathrow.

Once settled on to the train, Alex discovered that he had left his camera behind at Anne's. This was not to be the last time over the years when Alex was to leave behind some vital piece of equipment, but it set the scene for many future occasions. Always for him the important thing was to get moving, whereas for me I continually checked that I had everything with me. I have often wondered if many other wives found that their husbands suffered from a similar propensity, or whether it was just something my particular man was prone to.

The flight was uneventful and we were met at Bilbao by Paul and Clara. The parts of the city through which we drove seemed very drab, as we passed through streets like canyons lined with multi-storeyed blocks of flats bedecked with washing, but soon we left Bilbao behind eventually stopping at a charming seaside town called Laredo. Here we went to a café, well known in the area, where wonderful confections were served in splendid surroundings overlooking the sea. Afterwards we went to visit a chapel on a promontory with the most beautiful stained glass windows. Continuing our journey we finally turned inland towards Escalante and Clara's home. The village was approached by a narrow road lined on both sides by tall lime trees whose dappled trunks and overhanging branches made it seem as though we approached through a tunnel. Then we came to the village itself. The roadway was cobbled and rough and wood-railed balconies with the last of the summer flowers garlanding them leaned out over the narrow street. As we got out of the car, the air was strong with the smell of cattle as a neighbour's house also doubled as a byre for several cows.

Alex and me at the top of St. Mary's Lighthouse, Whitley Bay, Northumberland.

Dene Cottage after we had renovated it.

Cathleen, Bobby and me with our trailor tent.

The chalet in the snow at Meopham.

The family on the beach in Majorca. *Left to right;* Alex, Paul and wife Clara and daughter Laura, daughters Anne and Cathleen.

Alex and me and my children at my 60th birthday party. *Left to right, back;* Alex and me, *Front;* Cathleen, Chris, Paul and Anne.

Alex and me ready to enjoy our retirement, July 1990.

Alex with the Zulus at Shakaland, Natal, South Africa.

Clara's parents were waiting for us. The lower storey of their house was given over to storage, but I assumed that at one time it had also been a home for domestic animals. We climbed the narrow stairs and were welcomed into a small sitting room at the front of the house, crammed with dark furniture and well-padded sofas.

After a welcoming drink we were ushered into the dining room next door where a splendid meal was served. We later learned that the family meals were generally taken in the kitchen where Clara's mother cooked on a wood stove, but for today we were treated as honoured guests while she served us all, not sitting down to eat herself.

A few years older than Paul, Clara was the only child of her parents and although they would have liked more, it had not happened. Clara had been educated at the local convent and she showed me the beautiful bed linen and tablecloths she had embroidered with her initials in preparation for having a home of her own one day. As Spanish women retained their maiden names when they married, the choice of initial did not present a problem.

Clara's father, Enrique, was a builder and had built several houses in the area. It seemed that we were to be housed in one he had built and which was currently vacant. So after our meal we were driven there and soon settled down to a good night's sleep.

The village of Escalante was quite small with its street of old houses but it had a church and a small shop which sold everything. The next morning, Paul and Clara were to go to the Marie in Santander where their civil marriage would take place, so as we were to cater for ourselves apart from the occasional main meal, we walked to the shop to buy what we needed. No doubt we stood out like a sore thumb among the villagers, but also there was little doubt that they all knew who we were. We found it quite easy to point to most of what we wanted to buy, until I looked for some butter.

There didn't seem to be any on display that I could point to, and trying the French word did not seem to elicit any understanding. Eventually an onlooker was able to help and we discovered that the word we were looking for was *mantequilla*, which I would never have guessed in a thousand years.

As we made our way back through the village we met up with Clara's mother Luca, who took us to see the village washplace. This was a large square building with a roof but open sides and broad steps down into the water that ran through it. One or two women were there doing their washing in time-honoured style with hard soap and loads of elbow grease. Luca later told us, via our interpreter Clara, that occasionally she still took her washing there, although she had a perfectly good modern washing machine. Obviously, to use the public washplace would be more of a social occasion, as sometimes happened in our launderettes at home at a time when not everyone had an automatic washer or a dryer.

Later that day, Luca and Enrique came with Paul and Clara and gave us a tour around the immediate area. We went to see a house that Enrique was in the process of building for one of his nephews. It was built in the style that seemed to be the norm there, with the upper part of the building as the living quarters and the lower part without walls, only the supports springing out of the ground and a small central part bricked in where presumably the utilities would be housed for the rooms upstairs. They were in the process of tiling the kitchen with lovely glistening blue tiles while of course all the floors were well tiled. We then went to a piece of land that they owned where, at some time in the future, they planned to build a larger more modern house for themselves. The ground was covered with mature fruit trees and we picked ripe figs and ate them on the spot. Delicious!

Next day we went with Paul, Clara and her mother into Santander to collect her wedding dress. In the shop she went to try it on and I couldn't help tears springing into my eyes when she came out of the fitting room looking so slim and lovely. The dress was quite simple and fitted, and she would wear it with a long veil and a simple headdress.

Next it was to the shoe shop where Alex and I said we would wait outside. Probably a big mistake. Over the years we discovered that, once in a shop, Clara could linger indefinitely, but we were amused by a gentleman who came up to us and introduced himself in English, saying that he could tell we were English and would we mind if he spoke to us as he didn't get many chances to speak the language. It would have been hard not to guess that Alex was English as he always insisted on wearing his hat and his crombie overcoat, but we were happy to chat and it helped to pass the time. Santander seemed a gracious city with a wide paved centre with fountains and gardens and after coffee in a large café, we set off back to Escalante.

The wedding was not for another two days, so the next day we were picked up and were driven to see a fourteenth-century village called Santilla del Mar. We strolled through its narrow street of ancient houses with overhanging balconies and ochre-coloured walls. It was hard to tell if anyone still lived there, so quiet and deserted it seemed. At the far end we reached a rough road that curved round to the left and we were told we were going to see the caves where prehistoric paintings had recently been discovered by a herd boy. As we approached there was nothing to indicate the presence of a series of caves. The ground sloped slightly but there was no sign of any large opening, which I suppose was why it had lain undisturbed for so long. We were taken in and shown around by torchlight and as we went further in we became aware of figures painted on the walls, stick-like men with spears and various animals. At one point we were invited to lie back against a large boulder in the centre of the available space and view above us the large drawing of what could have been a buffalo or similar large animal. We gazed in awe at this work that humans had done many thousands of years ago and which we were now privileged to see.

We came out stunned by the experience. Now, a fourteenth-century village seemed very modern. The place was called Altimira and not long afterwards we heard that the caves were closed to visitors as the condensation caused by many people was damaging the paintings. Later, a reproduction cave was set up for anyone to see, but it could hardly equal the breathtaking sight of the real thing.

The night before the wedding, we were all taken on a hair-raising drive over a hilly road which led, we were told, to a fishing village in the next bay which was famous for its paella. At that time this was something we had yet to experience so we were full of anticipation. The restaurant was in an old building where we went down several steps into what felt like a basement with rough walls and uneven floors. We sat down at a long rough wooden table and placed before us were dishes of plump olives, baskets of chunks of bread and large jugs of red wine. The meal started off with dishes of seafood for all to pick at, small mussels, cockles and pieces of squid eaten with the aid of toothpicks and washed down with the splendid local red wine. Then at last, the pièce de resistance, a large steaming dish of fragrantly spiced paella, the rice lightly coloured by the saffron and decorated with crayfish and large prawns. Within its depths were chunks of chicken and mussels still in their shells. We were each given a bowl and our host stood and dished out generous portions to everyone. What a feast!

The day of the wedding arrived. The air was cool after a recent rainfall and, dressed in our best, we drove up into the hills to the monastery. The church stood on a hilltop with splendid views around the surrounding countryside, and we and all the guests, unlike English weddings, waited outside the closed doors for the bride to arrive. Paul looked smart but understandably nervous, probably as nervous as I felt, as it had been explained to me that Clara would go in first accompanied by her father, and that Paul would follow accompanied by me. So that instead of sitting behind as an interested bystander, as it were, I would be a large part of the wedding party and at some point would be involved in the responses.

At last Clara arrived, looking lovely in her dress and carrying a spray of five red roses. The church doors opened and she entered first with Enrique followed by Paul and me, after which all the other guests piled in and took their places in the body of the church. We four, however, were placed in the centre seats in front of the massive altar. The church itself was magnificent. The wall behind the altar was filled with gilded statues while high above in an alcove was a small figure of the Virgin Mary dressed in robes of blue.

The service began and behind us the congregation made the required responses which I of course could neither understand nor repeat. The biggest problem was knowing when to stand, when to sit down, and when to kneel, and I suspected that Paul was as much at sea as I was, so I had to content myself with trying to keep a weather eye on Clara and Enrique and follow their lead.

Alex, meanwhile, had been loaned a camera by Paul which he had loaded up with a fresh film, and as it seemed that photo-taking was quite acceptable he had joined the wedding photographer at the side of the altar and was snapping merrily away.

After the service the priest led the bride and groom, followed by us and then the rest of the congregation, to a small door let into the back of the building at the side of the altar. We found ourselves in a high-ceilinged open area with a flight of stone stairs leading upwards to a small platform and then down on the other side. Climbing this, we found that we were at the back of the alcove holding the Virgin Mary, where everyone bent and kissed her robes and of course we followed suit.

At last we all left the building redolent of the smell of incense and walked out into the freshness of the mountain air. Above us was the modern restaurant where the reception was to be held and we all trooped gaily up the rutted road and into a large room where champagne was served before we entered the main area.

At last large double doors were flung open onto a dining room set with many tables and we, along with the rest of the main wedding party, were seated at the head table. There followed a meal the like of which we had never seen before. Course after course was set before us: fish, meat and rice dishes culminating in the cutting of the wedding cake, a many tiered confection of sponge cake with a meringue-like coating. Wines were plentiful and the noise levels in the room rose to extreme levels as the Spanish guests did what they liked best – talking at full volume and when necessary, shouting above the din.

Dancing took place in the bar area until eventually the happy couple left for a honeymoon of a few days. We returned at last to the house. A day or two later we drove back to Bilbao and caught our plane home, but not before Alex discovered that the camera Paul had lent him, and with which he had so assiduously taken lots of photos, had not in fact taken any at all. It seemed that the film Paul had put in had not rolled on between the shots as it should.

Back in England we collected Bobby from Anne in Croydon, then set out on the long drive home. Although some of the M1 motorway was available to help us along, much more of the journey took longer on the A roads and we were glad to arrive safely back after our wonderful experiences.

11

Now that he had no job to come back to, it was imperative that Alex find something as quickly as possible. We bought the local newspaper, and one night he saw an advertisement for postal workers and promptly wrote to apply for the job. Before long he was called for an interview and found that the person interviewing him was a man who lived near us and who was a manager at the Sunderland office. He said he had called Alex in as he was curious as to why a neighbour should be applying for what seemed a fairly lowly job. So Alex explained how he had come to be jobless and was promptly taken on.

We met up in town after he had been in to get all the details of his new employment and were astonished at the rates of pay and the overtime available, and all paid for, unlike all the hours he had put in as a Pools Organiser without payment. At last, after a rocky start, we felt that now he had a steady job and, knowing what a good worker he was, I had no doubt that he would do well. It wasn't long before he was taken off foot deliveries and put onto van driving and delivering. Although the hours were long and started at an unearthly time in the morning, he did not mind and enjoyed his job.

As winter approached, Cathleen wanted to attend a Salvation Army Sunday School in town so every Sunday afternoon I would drive her there and drop her off. Then I would drive further along the coast with Bobby, and after parking the car near the beach, we would enjoy a brisk walk along the frozen edge of the sea as the waves crashed hard upon the shore. Those moments were very special for me, they were so different from the life I had led in the heat of South Africa not so very long ago and I could look back and see how far the family and I had come in a few short years. Soon it would 1976 and eight years seemed to have flown by.

The house felt empty with my three elder children all making their own lives and, as is so often the way, all of them were so caught up in the process that we only occasionally heard from them. But I was proud that they were all turning out to be independent and ready to stand on their own feet without looking for any help from the older generation. Not that we could have done much, but in an emergency we would have done what we could.

Poor Alex, however, took a very hard knock from his daughter. She was engaged to a young man called Kim who had recently graduated from university with a BA and was working for a leading soap manufacturer in Newcastle. She and Kim came to call on us with the express purpose of telling Alex that they were to marry, but that unfortunately they did not feel it would be appropriate for him to attend the wedding due to the acrimonious nature of her parents' divorce. Alex was devastated as, despite all, he had hoped to lead his daughter down the aisle at her wedding, but it was not to be. We sent a sizeable cheque but failed to get an acknowledgement.

The exercise down on the deserted and freezing beach after a week cooped up in an office was good for me and Bobby's little legs would carry him far and wide as he roamed the shore chasing up interesting smells. We did not go to the cottage during the winter months as sudden snow-falls could result in us being stuck there, perhaps for several days.

In January of 1976, Anne had had her second child, a son named Christopher, and as I couldn't get away at that time we suggested that they come and visit us and stay at the cottage in the summer.

As spring approached we began again to look at the garden with critical eyes. The previous owner had done nothing at the back which was the larger part, stretching out at the end of the cul-de-sac. Alex had decided to have a vegetable garden on the left with a lawn and a water feature in front of the French doors from the house. We now bought a rotovator and in no time had planted a good selection of vegetables and at the same time he began to dig out the pond. At the side of the house we erected a greenhouse and filled it with tomato plants, while along one side of it we planted strawberries, which that summer had almost more fruit than we could cope with.

At the weekends we were able to go to the cottage again and we would scour the hills for likely-looking stones to bring back for rockeries and to make a waterfall. There was such satisfaction to be had from making plans and working hard together.

We still went up to Newcastle to visit Auntie Maryon every week. The house became more and more noisesome as she failed to do any cleaning and gradually retreated from the main living room to more or less camping out in the drawing room. There we would sit crouched before the fire on furniture covered in dog hairs while she went off to the kitchen to make tea and to bring out the cherry cake she always bought from Marks and Spencer, as she knew it was Alex's favourite. We always partook of whatever she produced although I shuddered to think of the state the kitchen was in.

One evening we noticed a framed photo of a couple with a small child displayed on the china cabinet. I did not recognise them but when Maryon saw me looking at it, she lifted it down and handed it to me. I knew I had never seen the woman and child before, but then she told me that the man was Louie. I could hardly contain my shock for he was almost unrecognisable. The well-padded features had disappeared and the eyes were sunk deep in their sockets; he was suffering, so she told me, from pancreatic cancer and had not much longer to live. The woman was the one he had moved in after me and this was their child. I was stunned as he had always prided himself on his fitness and this must have come as a terrible shock to him. A few months later we heard that he had died, but I found it impossible to mourn him in any sort of way. It was a part of my life which was now a closed book.

Later that year we received an invitation from my old school friend, Stella, to her twenty-fifth wedding anniversary. She and her husband Jack were having a disco at a hall near where they lived in Fenham, a suburb of Newcastle and we had a splendid evening. We were introduced to some of Jack's friends who, to a man, seemed to have taken early retirement from their jobs as lecturers at the university. It seemed that the stresses of teaching were more than could be coped with, but I was able to give them a tip about their benefits telling them that if, instead of claiming their retirement pension when they reached the age of 65, they continued to claim invalidity benefit for a further five years as they were entitled to do, then that would be a tax-free income which retirement benefit would not be. They all seemed suitably impressed.

It was my first experience of a disco and I was almost tempted to ask our hostess if the sound could be reduced a little. Fortunately I didn't, as I later learned the high decibels were part of the action. One could only feel concern for the hearing of future generations if this is what took place on a regular basis!

At the rear of our house there was what was euphemistically called a utility room, but the concrete floor was uneven with a cupboard built into the far wall. We began to think that we could improve on this and build a more useful extension. My Scottish friend at work had had an extension put on to her house and she invited us to go and see it, as she felt she could recommend the builder. We were impressed with the work so set about employing an architect to design a suitable layout. She finally came up with a plan which would give us a large dining area at the back of the garage with a bow window facing out onto the back garden. Along the side of the garage was a larger utility room with space for a chest freezer and washing machine, and with a toilet and shower room attached. The work went well and when it was completed we held a big lunch party with the aunts, Alex's mum and stepfather, and Paul and Clara who were visiting us at that time.

One of the problems at the office revolved around the annual leave chart. Separate charts for each management level were circulated early each year with the first choice going to senior staff. As I was a relative junior, I would find that the plum periods, that is, the days following on a public holiday, had already been hijacked. As these periods were usually also school holidays, I was never able to have any time off when Cathleen was off school, as one senior EO had a wife who was a teacher, and the best friend of an older female EO was also a teacher. When I complained of the unfairness of this system I was told that I would have to wait until I had the necessary seniority myself before I could put my name down for those dates.

Paul and Clara were living in a rented flat in the village of Col den Rabassa between Palma and the airport. Paul was now working for Dan Air and they suggested that we might like to come and visit them as, being Paul's parents, he could arrange for us to have free flights. This seemed too good an offer to miss, so I was able to book a couple of weeks between the holiday periods and we took Cathleen out of school. Once more we drove to Anne's house in Croydon taking Bobby with us to be looked after while we were away. It was also a good opportunity to see Claire again, whom we had not seen since coming down for her christening earlier that year, and to meet up with our new grandson, Christopher.

Claire was turning into a lovely child, with blue eyes and blonde hair, and Anne was obviously revelling in being a mother. I was not too sure about Dave, though. His driving school business was doing well but he expected Anne to stay home all the time to field the phone calls and arrange the lessons. In addition, he was out every night giving lessons until 9 pm so she was left on her own for a large part of the time. However, it wasn't for me to express my concerns, and I realised with a new business someone had to man the phones, so it was probably unavoidable.

We took the train to Gatwick and went to the Dan Air enquiry desk where tickets were waiting for us. However we were told that, as these were seats which would have stayed empty during the flight, right up to the moment of boarding, if someone else came along with a ticket which had been booked and paid for, we would not be able to fly. So it was a nerve-racking time as we checked in, went through passport control and after visiting the duty-free, made our way to the boarding gate.

But at last we were on the plane and as we took off I held Alex's hand tightly, as take-off and landing still terrified me after my close call so many years ago as I landed at Nairobi with Cathleen. On that occasion we had circled the airport before landing, with fire engines and ambulances racing alongside the runway as it had not been clear whether or not the front wheel of the plane had been locked in. Thankfully, all was well, but it was to be many years before I could fly without the palms of my hands being drenched with sweat. However I did discover that, although not normally one to drink spirits of any kind, a stiff brandy and ginger worked wonders.

On this occasion we were soon landing at Palma airport and as we were all marshalled onto the airport bus, suddenly I was swept up into a bear hug by my son in a very smart navy uniform, much to the astonishment of the other passengers, no doubt. Soon we were through passport control again and had collected our luggage. Paul was still working so Clara was there to take us the short journey to their flat, which was quite spacious.

We had a lovely two weeks as they took us around the island. At that time the roads inland were rough and ready, often narrow and twisting and lined with shrubs and trees. Sometimes they led to secluded little beaches where we picnicked and drank cold white wine out of cool boxes filled with ice from the local garage. We visited the monastery in the northwest of the island and took the twisting road known as La Colobra down to a tiny beach at the bottom. Another trip was to another monastery, this time built upon the crest of a hill where, at Easter time, pilgrims made the winding journey up the steep road on foot.

The local restaurants were better than anything we had seen before, often with tables outside in pleasant gardens or on terraces looking out over the sea where splendid seafood was served. The town of Porto Cristo was unforgettable as the place where we visited the underground caves and floated across the subterranean lake in a boat while music drifted across the blue water. All too soon it was time to leave the lovely island of Majorca but it was certainly not to be our last visit over the coming years.

Anne and Dave came to visit that summer, as we had planned, with Claire now an active two-year-old and Christopher delightful at six months old. This was the summer of 1976, to be marked in people's mind as the first really sustainably hot summer experienced in this country almost within living memory.

Up at the cottage we drove into Alston and the whitewashed

buildings clinging to the slopes of the hill looked almost Italianate as they glistened in the sunshine, set against the brilliant blue sky. Up in Nenthead the water in the streams coming down from the hills became lower and lower and the teachers brought the children out of the school to play and frolic in the sparkling water of the remaining pools in order to cool off. I felt so fortunate to be able to enjoy such lovely surroundings and to have a life where finally things had fallen into place. But nothing stays the same for long and as the year wore on, changes began to appear on the horizon.

That winter two things happened at work: we got a new manager, and I was moved from the short-term benefit section to oversee the pension section. This meant I also had a new HEO and instead of going away on a training course, I was introduced to the work by the EO I was replacing, a very nice Scottish girl who had moved to live in the area after meeting and marrying an electrician who worked down the mines. She had two daughters and had a continual battle with her weight which seemed to stay the same no matter what she ate. She was extremely clever and knew the job inside out, so I had a very good tutor. Part of the job consisted in adjudicating decisions from time to time and for this I had to go to London for a week's course. At that time the IRA had been bombing some of the cities and I was asked if I minded going. However, I considered the risk to be negligible. I went off by train the weekend before as I was staying with Anne and Dave and would be catching the local train from Croydon into Victoria every day then travelling by tube to Oxford Street to the offices we were using.

The course was uneventful and I was glad to return home again and take up my duties on the pension section. It was from this section that imminent retirees had their claim forms sent to them, prompted by a computer printout received in our office from the Central Office in Newcastle. Birth and marriage certificates would be authenticated and once all the details were verified and the necessary forms completed it was my job to sign that the pension would be awarded after fully checking a certain percentage. This all went back to Central Office where the order books were prepared and sent out.

A second benefit that we administered was death benefit for which the qualifying amount of National Insurance was a mere 25 weeks, so that apart from a death certificate the majority were paid without any problems. However, one day we received a claim from a widow and when we received the details of National Insurance payments from Central Office, to our astonishment her husband had never ever paid any insurance. Obviously this needed to be investigated in case there was some mistake, so an Inspector was sent out to interview the widow in a sympathetic manner. It transpired that the husband had earned his living by harvesting sea coal from the beaches south of Sunderland, where, after filling a couple of sacks, he would load them onto his bicycle and hawk it around the housing estates. Obviously he had earned sufficient for the needs of himself and his family, but now they would be dependent on their income from what could be paid to them from Supplementary Benefits.

Overpayments were another problem however, and did arise from time to time but were easily dealt with. On one occasion, however, a widow had continued to cash her husband's retirement benefit for some considerable time before notifying the Department of his death. The relevant letter was sent to her outlining the problem and asking for repayment, a letter which she promptly passed on to her solicitor. As such payments could legally be recovered from the deceased's estate, the solicitor was obviously the next person to contact. We sent a letter and when there was no reply I rang him up to explain the situation, because if he handled the estate it was his duty to check for any outstanding debts. Something which he obviously had not done.

When I was put through to him, he told me in airy tones that the estate had been settled and that no doubt his client had already spent the money! Somewhat nonplussed, I consulted the relevant Code, or book of instructions, where I found the section dealing with such an eventuality. There I discovered that all I had to do was to send all the details to a section at Central Office who had the legal expertise to tackle the solicitor and point out to him what his obligations were in the matter. In due course I received a letter of apology from him and a cheque for the overpayment. Whether he or the widow paid it, I never found out. Probably he had to.

Events on the national and international stage did not impinge greatly upon our life. Harold Wilson's unexpected retirement caused much comment of course, but as the reasons remained a closed book, the world moved on and 'Sunny Jim' Callaghan took over relatively seamlessly. The Patty Hearst drama came to a conclusion, Concorde made its first flight, and we began to hear more and more of the terrible starvation experienced in Ethiopia and Bangladesh.

At work, however, I felt that there was a climate change. Bit by bit it began to impinge upon me and eventually was to lead to a dramatic life change for us.

12

One of the things that had attracted me to the civil service in the first place had been that pay and conditions were the same for both men and women. However, I was now to discover that when it came to promotion, such equality might not be the case. As one HEO patronisingly said to me, 'I think that you married women have done quite well when you get to the EO grade.' As the man in question had obviously waited many years to reach the HEO grade himself, he seemed to think that women, while probably not being the main wage earner, should not be allowed to compete with their male counterparts.

At that time the lower Clerical Assistant, and Clerical Officer (CA and CO) grades were mainly held by women, while the higher echelons, certainly in our office, were only male so that the scales were weighted against any female daring to hope for advancement. For the younger girls this was fine and we had a continuous round of collections for engagements, marriages and then baby showers as one by one they left to start a family and were replaced by other young girls, with the very occasional young man putting in an appearance. So far I had been able to climb the promotional ladder with the aid of the examination system, but anything beyond that depended on being selected to go before a promotion board.

We had two young men who were EOs. One was not doing very well and was called in for a chat with the HEO in a bid to get him to pull up his socks. The interview failed to achieve its object, for when he came out of the meeting

137

it was with the understanding that he was actually doing very well, so lightly was he being let down. He had to be called back for another chat so that the bitter truth could be put to him.

The other young man had come in as a direct entrant having decided that teaching was not for him. He spent his days lounging back in his chair at the head of his section and telling any of his staff who came for advice to look up the answers for themselves. None the less, another of the HEOs commented about him, 'Must get him pushed on, young man like that.' Not long afterwards he left for fresh pastures, perhaps for somewhere where the work was not so onerous.

There was to be a big change in the way that some of the benefits were administered which would involve wholesale training across the board. A staff meeting was held with HEOs and the section EOs to discuss how to formulate a plan, which I attended. While endless discussion went on, I was sitting quietly thinking when a solution came to me. Asking if I could speak – a necessary ploy to cut through the rising decibels – I suggested that initially we should create a training section, take one person from each section, and train them. Once they were up and running, they would then train another person from each section after which they would go back to their section and the person they had trained would train the next one and so on, until everyone was trained. This meant that there was very little disruption in the normal work as only one or two people at a time would be missing from their section and everyone would be trained in a short space of time. This idea was hailed with enthusiasm by the HEOs and before the meeting was concluded no one was in any doubt that it had all been their idea in the first place. I later learned at a headquarters training session that this method had been used elsewhere and had had the name the Cascade System attached to it.

So in small ways I was made to feel sidelined and this

began to press on me. I was asked to train another recently promoted EO, a young woman who was to go to work at a neighbouring office, which I did with great pleasure. We got on well and before long I felt that she had got the hang of the job as she went off to take up her new appointment. But still I found that I was being criticised for small matters which were not my fault, so that I continually had to fight my corner, something I was not very good at.

About the same time a report was circulated into the comparative costs involved with the administration of the various benefits, and it appeared that the cost of administering the sickness and injury benefits were huge compared to the amount of benefit paid out. It did not take a genius to work out that before long an alternative to the system would be found and a year or two later so it proved, when the whole thing was handed over to the employers to take care of.

How do you pinpoint the moment when things seem to start to go wrong? Even after all these years, I am no nearer working out what the problem was. Up to now I had had no problems with my work wherever I had been and had got on well both with my colleagues and with those above me in seniority. Here I had run the sections I was in charge of without any difficulty and I was on top of my job. Yet I was conscious of a feeling of unease. The new manager was a strange man who rarely smiled and stalked around the office issuing, at times, strange orders about the general running of the place. Was it something I had said? Had I made some unguarded remark which had upset someone?

One day our HEO came onto the section and asked to take away the papers on a particular case. Later I was called to the manager's office where he sat with the HEO and with the papers in front of him. Somewhat mystified, I was then told that there had been a complaint from a recently widowed lady that her case had not been dealt with as it should. As I had not been given access to the papers I had no idea what had gone wrong, but it transpired that her late husband's death certificate had been sent in to the office and the relevant claim forms had been sent to her address. Several reminders were sent until it seemed a complaint had been made to the manager about the way her case had been handled. The reason we had had no reply was that the widow had gone to stay with her mother and neglected to tell us. This I only found out later when we got the records back, but at the time I had no way of defending myself and I was hauled over the coals in no uncertain manner. I returned to my desk in turmoil, wondering what was going on, but it made me realise that no matter how hard I worked, I was no longer fitting in at this office.

To my dismay, I began to find that whenever I was walking anywhere outside on my own, terrible swear words were going through my mind, words I would never have used under normal circumstances. Added to that I developed dark shadows and bags under my eyes, although I seemed to sleep well. My friend Betty suggested that we should go and attend yoga classes together, as she felt I looked run down and tired, so we did, and enjoyed them very much. But when even the yoga teacher commented that I looked tired, I decided that I had better go and see my GP.

I described my symptoms to him, including the swear words that ran unchecked through my mind, and after making sure that all my other vital signs were normal he said he thought I was suffering from anxiety state. He would give me a sick note and I should have at least two weeks off work. The idea of sending in a sick note with 'anxiety state' as a diagnosis horrified me. I knew it would spell the end of any hope of a career, and I pleaded with him not to put that on the sick note. But he was quite unsympathetic, saying that if I had a broken leg that was what he would put and as I had anxiety state, that would have to go down too. In addition he prescribed hormone replacement therapy and

140

Ativan tablets, an anti-depressant. Reluctantly I returned home and the initial two weeks off work extended into four. When I felt a bit better I spent a lot of time at the recently opened sports centre built in the middle of Sunderland, where I enjoyed the sauna and swam in the leisure pool with its waves, artificial beach and palm trees. Slowly the stress began to abate and we went up and re-opened the cottage after its winter sojourn. That Easter practically the whole of the country was basking in lovely spring sunshine but along the east coast and for several miles inland we were wrapped in a foggy mist, known locally as 'sea-fret'. The scientific explanation of this phenomenon is, I have been told, that as the earth warms up the air rises and cold air from across the freezing North Sea sweeps in and forms a thick mist. I stand to be corrected on this, but sufficient to say the effect was a blanket of fog for long periods of time. Luckily for us, when Friday evening came we could load up the car, Bobby making sure that he would not be left behind by hopping into the front as soon as he realised what was going on, and take off up into the hills.

Before long the mist would start to thin and we would break out into pale sunshine with clear skies dotted with fluffy white clouds. Arriving in Nenthead, we would unload the car and then stroll across the little footbridge over the chuckling stream and up the valley, breathing the cool fresh air and listening to the distant bleat of sheep with their lambs, the cries of the curlews circling above and the sighing of the light wind through the branches of the pine trees. Those wonderful weekends helped to alleviate the stress, and eventually I went back to the doctor and was signed off.

On my return to work, however, I knew that the damage had been done and I was kept very much at arm's length. I discussed it all with Alex and it seemed that the only solution would be to leave that office, one way or the other. It would not be easy but somehow, things had to change.

An advert appeared in the local paper for an administrator at the local British Gas office and as, when I enquired, their terms and conditions were not dissimilar to those of the civil service, I applied and was accepted for an interview.

The public counter was squeezed into a fairly small shop front, while behind it the office to which I was escorted was even more cramped, so that the interview took place in the open office surrounded by ongoing clamour. I felt it went well, but I was not comfortable with the set-up and a day later rang up and cancelled my application.

Again Alex and I talked through the possibilities, one of which would be to transfer to another office within the civil service. Every month what was called a 'D' circular came around with items on it of general interest along with advertisements for posts elsewhere. I took the next one home with me and we went through it together. At that time it was difficult to recruit more senior staff in the London areas, largely as the cost of housing was said to be so much higher in the south of England, but prices in the south had dipped somewhat within the last year or so. In addition any move came with a very healthy financial package to ease the transfer. But while it would be easy for me, it was less certain that Alex would be able to secure a transfer with the Post Office, a position he had no wish to give up.

When he made a few enquiries it seemed that it would indeed be possible for him to be transferred, so we began to treat the idea more seriously. The thought of London was quite attractive, as Anne lived in Croydon and we had made quite a few visits there so that the area was not entirely unfamiliar. Having made our decision I notified management of my intentions and they said they would support any application I made. So I began to apply for anything that came up which seemed to be of interest, until eventually I was accepted to fill a vacancy as an Inspector at a local office in central London, called the West End office, the move to take place in two months' time when our office was prepared to release me.

We immediately put our house on the market and at the weekends I set to and cleared out all the cupboards to make the final packing easier. Time was slipping by and we would be well into autumn before the move could take place, not always a good time to sell a house. In addition, we had to make a decision about the cottage. This would be the biggest wrench, but it would not have been practical to keep it as it would have stood empty for long periods of time and we certainly could not have driven so far to use it at weekends. It would be a great wrench to let it go after all the hard work we had put into it and with so many happy memories of our time spent there away from all the hustle and bustle of a big town. We felt we had no choice, however, and advertised it in the local Newcastle papers as the sale would have to be for cash. Meanwhile, I hired a van and my son Christopher and I went up and packed up all that we wanted to take with us, managing, with a great deal of puffing and panting, to squeeze it all in and close the doors.

Eventually we found a buyer, but were most amused to learn many years later that when the cottage was re-sold, he claimed that all the improvements had been undertaken by him.

Meanwhile, Alex, Cathleen and I travelled down to London, staying in Croydon, and began our hunt for a house. Anne and Dave lived in a suburb called Addiscombe, an area of older houses, but Dave drove us to a suburb called Shirley where there were spacious detached and semi-detached houses built on a slope and with extensive woods beyond them. The houses were well built and attractive and, as we decided we liked the area, we went to a local estate agent to see what was on offer.

The first weekend we were there we did not see anything that we liked, as the houses we were shown were on the

143

edge or just beyond Shirley. The only one within the area looked fine from the outside, but when we walked in the place smelled terrible and the rooms were dirty and untidy. So we left our details with the agent and before long we had a call to say that there were two now up for sale.

The first one seemed quite spacious but as we looked around the back Dave pointed out to us a lot a damp all along the rear wall, so feeling a bit doubtful we pressed on to the next one. This was a substantial semi-detached house with large bay windows and an oak front door. Inside, the large hallway had a cloakroom to the right under a staircase that curved up to the upper floor. The room at the front was a smaller dining room while the large back room was a living room with lovely double French doors leading out on to the back garden. The kitchen was a good size while upstairs were three double bedrooms and a bathroom and separate toilet.

We made an offer and after a bit of haggling, a price was agreed and we put it in the hands of our solicitor. We had had an offer on our own house, but shortly before we were due to move, the buyers withdrew. Fortunately, under the package to which I was entitled, bridging finance was available.

While all this was going on I had gone to start my new job, having left the Sunderland office without any regrets. The West End office, as it was called, was situated in Soho, just around the corner from the Berwick Street market, and as I did not know London at all I arranged to stay in a small family hotel near Paddington station. I travelled down by train at the weekend before I was to start and I was given a room at the top of the house with a small en-suite shower room. After all the turmoil of the past year I found that I revelled in it, enjoying a hot shower and climbing into the comfortable bed with a book and a hot drink The next day, Sunday, I wandered around a quiet London and in the early evening went into an almost deserted Indian restaurant and ordered a meal. It felt very strange to be so far from home and on my own, but somehow quite exhilarating.

The next day, armed with my A to Z, I made my way to the office, negotiating the route along the top of Carnaby Street of 1960s fame, where still the tourists roamed, and threading through the small back ways to reach Broadwick Street and Colquhoun House. Once there, I introduced myself and was taken up to see the Assistant Manager who then took me down to the training room and introduced me to the EO in charge of training. I was taken aback, however, to discover that the next day I would be expected to find my way to another training office situated in Acton, which I would be able to reach by catching a bus to Hammersmith. I left my hotel in good time and was able to check in at the new office by nine o'clock and meet up with several other hopefuls.

The job we were all going to do at a variety of offices was to deal with the fallout from the recent move away from paying National Insurance contributions by means of a weekly stamp to having a percentage of pay deducted at source. These sums were then sent to Central Office in Newcastle, where a lot of money had been invested in a computer system to apply them to each individual account and at the same time to do a ratio check to see if the correct amount had been deducted. The resulting chaos must have been staggering because hundreds of inspectors were now being recruited and trained in order to visit the employers and sort out all the payments which had fallen foul of the ratio check.

Having been trained on several benefits by now, the amount I had to learn about the contribution system was minimal, although for others with whom I was training it was felt necessary to include a wider range. The training was to last for four weeks, and on the first Thursday I was told to bring my overnight bag with me the next day as I would be allowed to leave shortly after lunch in order to catch the train back to Sunderland. I had spoken to Anne and Dave, and they offered

145

to have me stay with them which I was very happy with. I knew the expenses I received would be useful to them and I would be able to spend a bit of time with Anne in the evenings when Dave was out with his driving school pupils. Fortunately I had not brought many things with me so was able to pack up, pay for my hotel and leave the next morning.

Among the trainees at Acton was a girl called Jane Brown who was also to work at the West End office. Jane was a single lady who was well educated and had been trained as a Norland Nanny. Having successfully worked for several wealthy families, she had decided upon a change of career and had been accepted as a direct entrant into the civil service. Her father ran a transcontinental haulage business in Kent while her mother was suffering from bone cancer following from a protracted treatment for breast cancer. Jane shared a flat with a friend, Anna-Marie, in nearby Ealing and when, a couple of weeks into our training, it was announced that there would be a strike the following week on the London Underground, I knew I would be unable to travel to Acton from Croydon. Jane, generous soul that she was, offered to put me up in the flat for the couple of nights of the strike and so, complete with overnight bag, I stayed with them and slept on their sofa until the strike was over. Anna-Marie was a private nurse and was currently nursing a lady suffering from a debilitating wasting disease which was incurable. Anna-Marie was obviously a pillar of strength to the family, and some time after the untimely death of her patient, she married the husband, a doctor, and moved with him and his children to the West Country. Jane, meanwhile, adored her father, and worried endlessly as her mother struggled with her terminal illness. Jane was to remain a good friend and over the years was supportive of many friends undergoing much personal trauma.

So, until the purchase of our house was completed, I travelled between London and Sunderland every weekend, arriving late on a Friday to a meal cooked by Alex and leaving again on Sunday evening. Needless to say, it was with great relief that we were given a date for the completion of our house purchase. We booked our removal firm, saw all our goods packed up and set off to spend a night in a hotel until the van arrived the next day. I had no regrets about leaving Sunderland but was sorry to have to part from our good friends, Ted and Betty. We promised to keep in touch, and so we did, even up to this day.

Alex had been able to get a transfer to the Croydon sorting office, and we arranged a week's leave in order to settle in. Our furniture fitted in well: in the dining room my mother's sideboard and a lovely mahogany table that had belonged to Great-aunt Allie looked quite perfect, while the sitting room was spacious and took our comfortable chairs and occasional tables with ease. We had already made enquiries about a special school for Cathleen and she was able to get a place at a large school just south of the town. A special bus was to pick her up and drop her off at the end of the road so I had no worries about transport for her.

Alex started at the Croydon sorting office and we began to explore the surrounding area. The woods at the top of the street were an ideal place to take Bobby for his walks, but independent little character that he was, when Alex took him he preferred to walk on the other side of the road and pretend he was on his own. When we were living in Sunderland he went missing one weekend, and did not come back home until late at night. We were worried sick and toured the neighbourhood to no avail, until in the evening he returned, limping and covered in oil. We examined him closely and could find no injury, but of course we made a great fuss of him. To our amusement, ever after that if he had misbehaved and got a good telling off he would look sorry for himself, put an injured expression on his face and walk away limping.

My journey to work usually took an hour. If I left the

house just before 7 am I could catch a bus into Croydon, get off at the station and catch one of the many fast trains to Victoria. These took 20 minutes, then it was a rush to the tube, down the escalators and if possible, move down the platform to the point at which, when the tube stopped at Oxford Circus, the doors would open just where the upwards escalators were. A quick walk through the almost deserted streets and I could be stepping into the office at 8 am.

We both knew that the move had been a good one, my health improved and I loved the 'buzz' of working in central London.

13

Living in the north-east, we had become accustomed to the encapsulated areas of Newcastle and Sunderland where the perimeters of towns and cities were sharply delineated. Now we found that the suburbs of south London spread amoeba-like one into another. Norbury and South Norwood blended into Croydon, while off to the east of us the borders of West Whickam and New Addington were barely perceptible. But to the south of us, over the crest of the Shirley Hills, we soon discovered that we had easy access to lovely countryside around Biggin Hill and over towards Westerham and beyond, and spent many happy hours exploring our new situation.

I felt relaxed and ready for any challenge as we gradually settled in. The sale of the cottage went through and with the money we had gas central heating installed. When we bought the house it was heated by somewhat dated storage heaters, so that when we got up in the morning the house was too hot, but when we returned home in the evening the heat had all dispersed. The next task was to install a new kitchen as the old one was past its best. We agreed that Alex would strip out the old one, and the next day fitters came to put in the new one. Alex then tiled the floor and walls with lovely ceramic tiles.

Our final purchase was a Volkswagen Combi camper van in green and cream, and we had great fun shopping for an add-on tent and all the camping paraphernalia to go with it. We went one weekend to test it out at a nearby campsite and just loved the freedom and the sense of the outdoors that camping gave.

Not long after we had moved in, there was a knock on the door one evening, and two of our neighbours from a little higher up the street were on the doorstep. They asked me if I would like to join the local Townswomen's Guild. I was delighted, and a few evenings later they called to collect me and we walked to the local school where the monthly meeting was held. There was a good crowd of women, all much the same age as me, and I was made a member on the spot. Meetings were held every month with a speaker and other events from time to time. One year we went to the Windsor Rose Show and saw the Queen Mother drifting around the tent full of roses and in no mood to be chivvied along by her coterie of officials. It was a blazingly hot day and we all marvelled at the splendid flower arrangements set out in the tent of the Women's Institute all ready for the judging. It would have been hard to choose, so splendid were they all. As we strolled along the pathways, planes taking off from Heathrow roared overhead from time to time, seeming to barely clear the turrets of Windsor Castle. I was most amused to hear an American lady strolling in front of us remarking to her companion as she gazed up at the castle, 'You'd think they would have built it somewhere else, wouldn't you!'

A year or two later I took on the task of being Secretary to our branch of the Guild and later was Vice Chairman. I declined the offer to become Chairman, however, as I could not devote the time to it that would have been required.

Croydon itself was a good shopping centre, my favourite store being Allders, but there was also a big Debenhams as well as C&As, Woolworths, Littlewoods etc. For some time I used to buy fruit and vegetables at the Berwick Street market, almost crumbling under the weight of all I had bought as I staggered home on Tube, train and then bus, until we discovered the excellent market in Croydon where from then on we shopped on a Saturday. On the way home we would

150

call in to see Anne and the children and have a cup of tea with her. Claire and Christopher were leaving babyhood behind, another daughter Vanessa, had arrived to complete their family. In Majorca Paul and Clara had their first child, a little girl called Adella.

All in all, the move had been good for us all. Cathleen enjoyed her new school and the special bus picked her up at the end of the street and deposited her back again in the late afternoon, at which time I was usually able to be back home due to flexi-time and my early start. Alex settled well at the Croydon sorting office, although he did find that he was kept at arm's length by the largely south London staff. I was able to put behind me my unhappy experiences at the Sunderland office and settle into the happy family life that we all craved.

Once I had completed my training course I was introduced into one of the sections in the office. The error rate in the initial years of percentage deductions had been enormous and it was necessary to investigate every single ratio check which was thrown up as incorrect. Consequently, all the incorrect printouts for central London were sent to an office in Portsmouth where they were set up as individual files, except where several errors occurred for one employer. They were then sent to our office, known as the West End office, and our clerical section listed them, then sorted them into areas before they were recorded and passed on to us, the inspectors. We each had an area to deal with, the streets being listed within each area, and I was to have the Bloomsbury area.

Colquohoun House on Broadwick Street was a bulky 1930s building, part of which had been leased by the civil service especially for this task. Inside the entrance was a cubby-hole of a room complete with doorman who belonged to the building and had nothing to do with us. On the ground floor on one side was a large room housing the clerical staff and on the other, a room with a public counter and an outside entrance. The first floor had its own door into a corridor and here there were rooms with three separate sections of inspectors containing the ubiquitous arrangement of two lots of three steel desks facing another three desks. Each had another small room attached or adjacent for the HEO running the section.

The second floor was leased to a company which did voice-overs for TV adverts and it was not unusual to see famous people from time to time. Once I leapt into the lift in the rush to deal with some problem or other. Seeing a familiar face I happily said, 'Oh, hallo!' only realising as I got out on the next floor that it was John Mills. On another occasion, as I came down the stairs I saw Diana Dors in deep conversation with our doorman and another time I held the door open for Peter Bowles as he struggled in with his leg encased in plaster. All of this added to the charm and excitement of working in central London.

The third floor housed another three sections and their HEOs as well as the offices of the manager and his assistant manager. The staff were mainly directly recruited EOs either straight from university or having spent some time working, mostly as teachers it seemed, so that we had at least 70 people dealing with central London. To begin with, not knowing central London at all, I divided my area up into a lower, middle and higher area, each one served by a tube station, so the furthest north was Kings Cross with Russell Square in the middle and Holborn at the bottom, all on the Piccadilly line. In the course of time I became more used to the streets and found I could walk quite easily to the area nearest the office without having to dive down stairs and escalators and along endless passageways onto the Tube.

Each file had to be dealt with within a certain time limit, which meant keeping them in strict order in the desk drawer. At the same time we kept a running list of them all so that queries could be handled easily and quickly. Each Friday I would set up as many appointments as possible for the coming week, dividing them among my area as economically as possible, then packing the files into my civil service issue briefcase, I would set off to interview as many as possible. As well as the briefcase we were given a warrant with strict rules as to which premises we could, or could not, demand to enter. Afternoons were spent writing up the notes from our official notebook, not unlike a policeman's notebook, as if necessary it could be produced as evidence in any court case.

I soon got into the swing of things and gradually reduced the load that I had inherited, although it never seemed to run out. My area contained many of the hospitals and much of my time was taken up with trawling through the pay records at the Great Ormond Street Hospital for Sick Children and at the Hospital for Nervous Diseases. My bête noir, however, was the file for the Imperial London Hotels. For some reason when it had been assembled down in Portsmouth, instead of being made into several files of manageable proportions, the queries had all been lumped into one huge file containing over a hundred different checks. Any files that had been around for more than three weeks were listed by the clerical section and sent to the HEO to check, so that my Imperial London Hotels file was a regular visitor to his desk. Had I received the file initially myself I could have returned it and had it broken down into smaller units, but as it was it had already been started by my predecessor so I had no choice but to battle on. The wages office for the group of hotels was situated in a building in a side street, where the room was large and poorly decorated with holes in the carpet and heating provided by electric fires. The staff were older women but cheerful and I got on well with them. Because of the number of salaries to be checked for errors, I was there every week and even had a desk for my own use. Checking the file one day, the HEO called me in to report on progress then said, 'I suppose you enjoy a nice lunch while you are there!' If only! Certainly I was well supplied with cups of tea but the office itself was far away from the opulence of the Imperial London Hotels.

I found that this was not unusual, as on a visit to the upmarket store of Heals I passed through the warm and elegant store until through double doors I entered a draughty, warehouse-like domain along corridors and up metal staircases until the wages office could be found. On another and later occasion, when filling in for a colleague who covered the Berkeley Square area, I had occasion to go to Hartnell's, the Queen's dressmaker. Passing through the luxurious showroom with its platform where the mannequins strutted, I was taken by the back stairs through the workrooms. Here, very elderly ladies were busily stitching away or cutting materials at enormous tables, but we passed through and made our way up another even narrower stair to a small attic room with a tiny window looking out over the roof tops. Seated at a rough wooden desk was a woman wrapped up in several layers of clothing to protect her from the chill; light years away from the scene the customers would have seen below.

Our HEO was a strange man who told me that he had once been an EO in a local office when he had occasion to interview a lady who was recently widowed. He himself could not have been in the first flush of youth at that time, but it seemed that a relationship was established and eventually they married. He was never abashed to tell us all about his married life. It seemed when he arrived home he had to change out of his shoes and into his slippers. No big deal you might think, except that on going upstairs his wife felt it necessary for him to change into yet another pair of slippers, before proceeding to the upper floor. Often, to our puzzlement, he would come to the office carrying Marks and Spencer bags. While we could understand him leaving the office with bags, we found it odd that he arrived with them, until we learned that it was his wife's habit to shop at the local M&S store, but then change her mind and get him to return the goods to the store on Oxford Street, poor henpecked fellow!

The area where our office was situated was adjacent to Chinatown and to the area of strip clubs and shops selling sex aids. These areas were always covered by one of our male counterparts, mostly because the Chinese community refused to have business dealings with women. This was not an area where any of us women felt like pressing our claims to equal opportunities, needless to say.

Ruth, one of the girls on our section, dealt with many of the Greek restaurants in the area and often she would pick out a good one and we would all go there for lunch. Chop, short for Chopra, our Indian compatriot, took us all to experience the local Hare Krishna restaurant, while we had the choice of many Chinese and Vietnamese establishments. Thus my knowledge of many ethnic foods became more expansive, while shopping in the many delicatessens and specialist butcher shops was a delight and greatly expanded our menu at home.

After our first winter in the south-east, our summer holiday was taken at a campsite called Sandford just north of Wareham near the Isle of Purbeck. The site was large and well kept with a big swimming pool and excellent facilities, and we were able to set out each day and explore the surrounding area. We loved Poole and visited the pottery and some of the lovely gardens nearby. Our travels took us further west to Dorchester, Chesil Beach and the swannery at Abbotsbury, giving us an appreciation of parts of the country we had never before visited. The silent beauty of the Blue Pool and the charm of Swanage after passing the ruined grandeur of Corfe Castle were memories to be treasured.

On our return Alex set to remaking our garden with a vengeance. He re-laid and extended the paved patio outside our French windows, then set about constructing a fish pond beyond it. As the ground sloped very gently he did not dig too deep, but constructed a retaining wall enclosing one corner of the ground there, making a raised section at the back to take a waterfall. Once completed and stocked with pretty fish, it was a pleasure to hear the splashing water through the open doors on warm evenings.

Trips to Majorca were more easily arranged now that all we had to do was to catch the Gatwick train at Croydon which took us right to the airport, and we were able to go over and spend an occasional fortnight with Paul and Clara and their family. Additionally, now that I no longer came last in the pecking order as far as choosing when to take any leave, I was able to arrange for several small breaks throughout the year. With flexi-time, having put in the hours over a four-week period, it was possible to build up the occasional day off, which when linked to a public holiday and regular days of leave could result in a two-week break two or three times a year.

Paul and Clara had bought a flat in the village of Col den Rabassa, quite near Palma Airport where they both worked, Clara with a Spanish company called Barcello and Paul with Dan Air. His boss, a young man called Brian, was popularly known as Dougal. Whether this had anything to do with the name of the dog in the TV programme *The Magic Roundabout* I never found out, but the name stuck and was used by all and sundry, except for his lovely parents whom we often saw when they too were visiting the island.

On Friday nights the staff of Dan Air would congregate at their favourite bar in C'an Pastilla and we would often join them and listen to their hilarious tales. One favourite was when the company received a phone call from one of the package tour firms asking to book a PLD in a week's time. As the term PLD was a euphemism for Passenger Lying Down, in other words a body, they were a bit curious as to why it would not be transported for at least another week. On querying this they were told that the deceased, a lady, had been accompanied by her elderly husband, and he was having such a good time that he wanted to enjoy the rest of his holiday before taking his 'dear departed' back to the UK for burial!

On another occasion Paul, who by then could speak excellent Spanish, was dealing with the missing luggage of a young English girl. After sorting it out at some length in Spanish, he turned to the girl and explained the situation in English. Gazing at him with great admiration she said, 'Oh, you do speak such good English!'

Paul and Clara's new flat was in a narrow little street. The lower floor was owned by the builder and extended into a large garden below. The floor above was theirs, with three bedrooms, two bathrooms and a lounge with a large terrace from which the sea could be seen across the top of the fort. I have no idea of the historical significance of this fort, but it had been abandoned for many years and could be entered through huge double doors. Around it were stout walls and on the corners facing the sea gun emplacements had been dug in, reached by dark subterranean passages. The whole edifice was set in a large cleared space which youngsters on noisy mopeds used as a short cut.

We loved our visits there from the moment after landing, when the doors of the plane were opened and we stepped out into the warm and sometimes humid air before entering the airport itself. Compared with Gatwick the airport was spotless and beautifully tiled with gleaming marble. With free access behind the scenes because of working there, either Paul or Clara would be there to greet us and carry us off to their waiting car, while the bulk of the remaining passengers sorted out their courier and queued up for the buses waiting to take them elsewhere in the island. In 1980, their family had been increased by the arrival of Laura.

157

During our stay we would enjoy the small local beach each day and have a meal in one of the many small cafes along the front. We soon had our favourites and grew adept at ordering coffee or beer in Spanish. No big deal, perhaps, but we loved it and it made us feel a part of the country. When Paul and Clara had days off, we would load up the car and drive to one of the many lovely beaches up the east coast, at that time largely undeveloped. The coolbox would be filled with the small bottles of Spanish beer and a few of white wine before topping it up with ice from the local garage.

On Sundays we would go out for lunch and it never ceased to amaze me that we could travel for miles until we reached what seemed to be a deserted group of buildings next to a main road. On entering the largest one we would be assailed by the sight and sound of tables filled with the extended Spanish family, where you could hardly be heard above the roar of loud Spanish voices. As the menus were all in Spanish we generally left the ordering to Clara and so were able to savour many dishes which otherwise we would not have known of. Not far from where they lived was a military club for the use of soldiers doing their National Service, but where local people could also be members, so from time to time we all went there for a meal and to use the lovely swimming pool and other facilities. Returning home often felt like being forced back into a straightjacket of work and time-keeping, much as I loved my job.

Alex's daughter, Jacqueline, and her husband Kim were living north of London at Hemel Hempstead, quite a long and complicated drive in the days before the construction of the M25. We went to see them after the birth of their first child, a daughter called Geraldine, in the small starter-home they had bought. But once again Alex was disappointed when he was not invited to his granddaughter's christening.

We went back to Newcastle to see Alex's mother and my

aunts as often as we could, but we began to find that our camper van left a lot to be desired in the power department. Additionally, if there were strong crosswinds on the long drive through Yorkshire and Durham, it could be a battle to keep it on the road. On one occasion, travelling on a three-lane motorway, Alex would overtake a truck as our van went downhill, but on the drag up the other side of the rise he would lose power and have to drop back while the truck, a bakery van if my memory serves me right, overtook us. This went on for some time until the truck took an exit road off the motorway and we carried on. We had not gone far, however, before we were flagged down by a police car. Wondering what was wrong Alex pulled over, and wound down his window. The policeman asked to see his driving licence. He then questioned us closely as to our destination, all the while giving the interior a good looking over. All that could be seen, of course, was our luggage and the double bed which we always let down so that Cathleen could while away the hours of travelling.

He then began to laugh. Apparently the lorry driver with whom we had been playing ducks and drakes was carrying a substantial sum of cash back to his base and, thinking that we were setting him up for a robbery, he had taken our licence plate number, turned off the motorway and phoned the police! We had to laugh too, as it was the first time we had ever been suspected of being highway robbers.

14

Life was so much better since our move. The older children were settled, grandchildren were arriving thick and fast, I enjoyed my work and Alex and I were loving every minute of our lives. I began to wonder if I still needed to take the Ativan tablets, as I didn't think I could still be suffering from depression. So I stopped taking them, but in a very short space of time I began to feel unwell again. I was convinced I was no longer suffering from an anxiety state but it did occur to me that I may have become addicted to the tablets.

There seemed only one thing to do and that was to gradually reduce the dose and see what happened. I was taking one tablet three times a day, so I started off by breaking the mid-day one in two over the course of a week, and was pleased to experience no side effects. Over the next month I gradually halved the morning and evening tablets so that I was only taking half the original dose. All went well, so encouraged by the outcome I gradually left out the midday dose and eventually, the morning and evening one, so that I was free of the medication, without any side effects. A year or so later there was a quite a bit of publicity about possible addiction to these drugs, so I was pleased I had been able to recognise it for what it was, and take the necessary action.

Alex's mum had been struggling with her health for some time. The cancer had spread and she had had to undergo many painful types of treatment, none of which was proving to be successful. Eventually she refused anything further and we arranged to travel up to Newcastle as her condition deteriorated, but we were too late and she died at home not long before we arrived. I could only imagine what that poor soul had gone through. Ossie took me through to her bedroom where her tiny shrivelled little body lay waiting for the undertakers. She had been a wonderful woman and a mother-in-law that anyone would have been happy to have. Her family were her sole concern and she cared for her husband and ran his home with dignity and economy, making their pension stretch much further than many might have, while always setting a table with nourishing and well-cooked meals. I was proud to have known her and glad to have counted her my friend. She had accepted Cathleen as an additional grand-daughter, and Cathleen had loved her too. We stayed on in Newcastle for her funeral before sadly returning home again.

Not all our work was with payrolls and ratio checks. Many of the files we received related to self-employed people who had neglected to buy their stamps for their self-employed National Insurance card, the only area of National Insurance which was still administered by a standard weekly payment. Round Brunswick Square there were several blocks of council flats where men running a small business as an electrician or perhaps a plumber lived. It was almost impossible to get hold of these fellows, as obviously they left early for work, and even if I sent a letter asking for an appointment at a specific time they had little incentive to keep it. After a bit of thought I hit on a strategy. Leaving home a good half-hour earlier than usual, I could arrive on my patch unannounced at round about 8 am. It seldom failed and I was able, usually quite amicably, to explain to a pyjama-clad fellow that he really had no choice, short of a court case, but to pay up and keep his cards up to date.

These council estates were very well kept but others

161

weren't, and after a visiting civil servant had been brutally murdered elsewhere in the country, we all had to go on a course giving us advice on what to do when visiting a private home. We were taught to recognise the signs of aggression and to make sure that, once inside the house, we positioned ourselves to ensure an easy exit. One visit I had to the less salubrious area for which I was responsible had to be done on a dark winter's evening, so with my HEO's permission my pal Chopra went with me, and all went well. Generally speaking, though, there was never any danger although calling in to some of the sleazy hotels near Kings Cross where rooms were hired by the hour was only ever undertaken in the full light of morning.

Local offices who had been unable to get a reply to their letters of enquiry would also send a file, and I once had to visit what was supposed to be a doctor's surgery. After some hunting around I found it stuck in the basement of a high-rise block of flats. The doctor, a woman, looked as if she had seen better days and her grubby ill-lit office seemed as though it had not had a good clean for many a long year. I had been asked to check the medical records of one of her patients, but looking around it became obvious that record keeping was the last thing on this lady's mind. She could not even recall the name of the patient, so for once I had to come away without a result. The file was returned to me by the local office a little while later as they found it hard to believe nothing could be found. I described her 'surgery' as best I could. I could only suspect that she had something to do with the drug-taking community, but it was not up to me to say how she should, or should not, run her business.

Collecting arrears of self-employed contributions could often be a headache. One man in particular stands out in my memory. He was the owner of a rather run-down little Indian restaurant and had neglected to pay for two or three years. I would send an appointment card with a time to

162

coincide with my next visit to the area, only to be told by his monosyllabic waiter that he was not there. This went on for some time, until in exasperation, I went in, sat at one of the tables and put my government-issue briefcase down on the table with a flourish. Next thing the waiter scurried off and in no time arrived back, hotly followed by his boss. We then sat down while he spun me a long tale of troubles and setbacks which I duly wrote in my notebook. I was entitled to give him exemption from payment if I judged we were unlikely to get the money, so I made the necessary arrangement and issued him with a new card for stamping from then on. As I was leaving I warned him that non-payment would not only result in a court case, but would also affect the amount of pension he would be entitled to draw when he was 65. At that his whole demeanour changed and he followed me out of his premises begging me to reconsider, because amazingly he was now sure he could find the money for the back payments. But it was too late, although I expect that from then on he ensured his card was kept up to date.

The next summer Alex and I decided to have a go at taking our camper van to France. The French Tourist Board had a splendid office on Piccadilly and I spent much time there looking at maps and using their extensive display of campsites and places of interest. Early one morning in June, as the morning mists gradually cleared from the fields, we bowled along the Kent roads to the port of Dover. We had never been on a cross-Channel ferry before so were fascinated at the way the various shapes and sizes of vehicles were marshalled on the docks before being waved forward and slotted into the most economical space on the decks. With great excitement we mounted to the upper decks and ordered some breakfast, and in no time at all Cathleen, Alex and I were standing at the rail watching the coast of France appear through the sunshine. This is not a travelogue so I will not detail the joys of that holiday, but we were charmed by the Breton towns and countryside and the little box-like black and white houses that seemed to fill the hillsides.

On our return in the early hours of the morning, we stopped at an all-night filling station not long after leaving the ferry. Hearing my husband's Geordie accent, the cashier jokingly commented that we still had a long way to go before we got home, to which Alex was delighted to reply that on the contrary, we would be home within the hour.

Emboldened by our trip, we decided to have a week's holiday in Paris. In the streets behind Buckingham Palace was a company called Paris Travel which specialised, as its name suggested, in trips to Paris. It was possible to book through them and travel by your own car, by air or by rail, so we decided to travel by rail. We caught the boat train at Waterloo Station and in no time were crossing the Channel once more, but this time we trundled across the plains of northern France on the train, where admittedly there was not a great deal to see. At the Gard du Nord we caught a taxi to our hotel which was not far from the Sacré Coeur. It was not what one could call luxurious, but as we only intended to sleep there it did not matter. At least it was clean and part of the deal was a continental breakfast every morning. We had also been given meal vouchers and a list of participating restaurants, so next morning we set off to the tourist offices near the Opera House where we were able to make our choice of tours. Versailles of course, as well as a trip on a Baton Rouge, were not to be missed, while on foot, long walks around the centre took us to Notre Dame and the Louvre and, my fear of heights notwithstanding, an ascent of the Eiffel Tower. The place I enjoyed the most, though, was Fontainebleu, set in beautiful countryside, where inside the pattern on the marquetry floors mirrored the designs on the ceilings.

Two things happened that amused us. One day we were

walking along the road where all the strip clubs were, looking for postcards, when we were loudly hailed by of all people our nextdoor neighbours! Neither of us had known we were to be there at the same time, but when I told Clara this tale some months later she was appalled and said *she* would have known if her neighbour was making such a visit. I'm sure she would, but that just shows how we British tend to mind our own business. As we all commented at the time, wasn't it fortunate that we were there with our respective husbands and wives. The other thing that brought a smile to our faces was when we were waiting to be seated at a typically French restaurant complete with waiters in long aprons, mirrors on the walls and the wonderful aromas of good French cooking. Behind us, two young American girls sidled in and to our surprise asked if they could be directed to the nearest McDonalds. Well, I ask you, why go to Paris and eat at McDonalds?

We made regular trips to Newcastle to catch up with friends and relatives. There were always several people to see but we made time to call in on my cousin Bill and his wife and their son and daughter, as well as our good friends Ted and Betty down in Sunderland.

Chris and Maggie had been living in a rented furnished flat in Gosforth, but decided to move into a slightly cheaper one as they were saving up to buy a house. After completing his baking and confectionery course, Chris had eventually gone to a well-known distributor of catering equipment and asked for a job. They had taken him on initially to work in the storeroom so that he could learn about all the stock, but now he was 'on the road' as a salesman.

Maggie had taken her teacher training course in Newcastle but when she graduated she had been a victim of the sudden drop in school entrants, following the widespread availability of the contraceptive pill. When she had gone to the Labour Exchange, as it was commonly known at the time, they lost no time in recruiting her for work on the other side of the counter. In the course of time Maggie and Chris bought a solid semi-detached house in one of the western suburbs of Newcastle and began to plan their wedding. The house was on a slope and was one of many built just before the war. I couldn't help thinking that my father had probably supplied the sand and gravel for the builder through his business as a builder's merchant.

Thus it was that, in 1981, all the family in the south-east drove up the motorway to Doncaster to attend Chris and Maggie's wedding in the cathedral at Doncaster. It was a lovely occasion and Maggie's mother had arranged a reception at a local hotel. Paul and Clara came as well, with their daughters Adella, now an active toddler and baby Laura. Clara distinguished herself by throwing a fit of hysterics when Adella fell down and grazed her knee, but as we said at the time, she is Spanish, isn't she. No harm was done and Adella's tears soon dried up.

Settling into their new home, Chris amazed us all by doing his own re-wiring, putting in central heating and building an extension to the kitchen which included a nice French door out into the garden. In 1984, their first child, Sarah, arrived and Maggie gave up work.

After our experience with our camper van, we decided we needed something with a bit more horse power, so we sold it and the tent which could be attached to it, and bought a Volvo estate car. We then had great fun choosing a trailer tent, having decided against a caravan mainly because the local bylaws would have prevented us parking it in our drive, but also we felt the lower height would make a trailer tent easier to tow. We discovered a wonderful purveyor of camping equipment near the Tolworth roundabout. Much of the other equipment we had used in the camper van was useable, but it was still a pleasure to trawl the shelves and add all sorts of refinements. Packing up for a holiday became a mammoth task and I would be making lists for days beforehand to ensure that nothing was left behind.

Our first foray with our new-set up was to the Dordogne, and we took Cathleen and Claire with us. The campsite was set up on a hillside with splendid facilities, and as we had brought an inflatable boat with us Cathleen and Claire, our eldest granddaughter, had great fun on the River Dordogne.

The following year we went across France to the Jura area, sited along the border of Switzerland. The campsite was at the head of a cirque, a blind valley surrounded by high cliffs and with a lake in the centre. Our site was right on the lake and it was magical to wake early in the morning, and see the fishermen out on their small boats almost concealed by the early morning mist. Later in the day windsurfers took advantage of any small breeze and at night we would barbecue and watch the sun setting behind the hills. Where we had our kitchen, we noticed that the legs of our chairs seemed to be dropping into holes under the ground sheet. This puzzled us somewhat, especially as there seemed to be something moving around. Eventually we cleared all the furniture out onto the grass and upon lifting the ground sheet we discovered that we were being undermined by moles. There was nothing to be done about it, but when seated at our table, whenever we saw a small upheaval at our feet we would stamp down hard in an attempt to dissuade them. When we finally left and packed our ground sheet away, we discovered a series of tunnels that would have put any escaping prisoner-of-war to shame.

The surrounding countryside was filled with forests, lakes, streams and waterfalls, and with caves which could be accessed above the water rushing out of them. On one day we travelled over the Swiss border to Geneva and saw the huge spout of water which shoots out of the lake, at that time being used as the opening sequence of a TV series called *The Champions*. Certainly a holiday to remember.

Much as I loved the job I was doing – as one of the lads commented, it was almost like being self-employed as we could organise our days as we wished – I had not given up on gaining promotion to HEO one day. Meanwhile, I steadily gained seniority and crept up the incremental pay scale until I was on the maximum salary. I was then in line to 'act up' as HEO when any one of our eight HEOs was on holiday. This was great because, for the period of time I did it, I was paid the upper rate. Plus the work was not onerous, I knew enough about it to take it in my stride and the extra money was a welcome addition to our finances.

Meanwhile, Alex had been put in charge of the telegrams office at Croydon, but now that most people had a telephone,or easy access to one, most of the telegrams that were sent were jokey ones to be read at wedding receptions. So it was decided to close down that side of the Post Office work. Alex was promoted and put in charge of a small sorting office in Warlingham, just north of Croydon.

He enjoyed the work as he was left to get on with it free from any interference from the main office, but one afternoon I got home from work at about 4.30 and he was not there. Normally he arrived home about 2 pm after starting work before 5 in the morning, so at first I did not worry, thinking he might have gone to the local shop. But when time passed and he still had not returned I began to panic. There was no reply at the sorting office so I knew he had not been held up there. I phoned the police. They were very polite but said that they could not treat such a case as serious until he had been missing for a day or two.

I was just about to look up the phone numbers of the local hospitals when Alex arrived back home. My relief knew no bounds as I sat him down and asked for an explanation. Apparently a small minority of his staff had refused to do

168

a particular round for some reason, so he and his second-in-command divided the work between them and went out and delivered it all themselves. I made him promise that if ever that situation was to happen again, he would phone me and let me know. For him though, the task of seeing that the post went out was paramount, and he took his responsibilities very seriously.

15

In the spring of 1984 we flew to Majorca to stay with Paul and Clara once more, as we preferred the lovely spring time when all the roadsides were a colourful display of wild flowers and the pink almond blossom covered the trees. However, staying with Paul and Clara was getting to be a bit crowded, as in 1982, a little grandson named Pablo had been added to their family. We had begun to feel that it wasn't fair to have to uproot one of the children from their room to make space for us.

One day as we were walking along the promenade near their home, I noticed that extensive work was being done to upgrade the area. The local beach, which previously had been very sparse and rocky, had been made into a lovely sandy beach protected by two rocky groynes stretching out into the bay, and a new promenade was being built all along the coast towards Palma with rows of palm trees planted along it. Things were obviously looking up. I turned to Alex and said, 'I think we ought to think about buying a flat here.' To this day he insists that he had been saying this all along and I hadn't liked the idea. Ah well. Whatever the truth of the matter, at least we were both agreed. Having said that, we didn't actually have any money, but such a stumbling block had never bothered us in the past.

As soon as we mentioned the idea to Clara she swept us off to look at newly built flats. I had really envisaged something quaint with flowering creepers around the windows, but in the real world that wasn't going to happen. One new development we went to see was on the seafront with a lovely view, but the sliding doors on the balcony failed to fit and the angle of the rooms was strange to say the least. However, off to the left of the area in front of the fort which Paul and Clara's flat overlooked, a building had recently been put up which at first I had thought must be a clinic or hospital of some sort, as the front was shielded by white louvred shutters. This, it seemed, was actually a block of flats and some of them were now up for sale.

Clara arranged for us to go and see what was on offer, so the next day we climbed the central flight of steps to the main glass door. On the landing before going in, there were doors to the left and right opening into the two ground-floor flats. These had been built so that their balconies were raised some few feet above the pavement level of the sloping road. We were ushered into the flat on the left which the builder was then using as his office, and once the door was opened were astonished to find ourselves facing an extensive terrace about 15 feet wide, running the length of the building. This was what lay immediately behind the louvred shutters, which could also be folded back in their entirety. Along the inner right-hand side there were a series of sliding glass and aluminium doors giving access to the main rooms. In the centre the double sliding doors opened into a large room which was the one being used as an office, with on the right a door into the kitchen, or what would be the kitchen. As was the custom with new builds, we would have the kitchen units built to our specification and although not large, it would be big enough to hold all the appliances we would require. It also had a smaller sliding door onto the terrace.

Back in the lounge, two thirds of the way along each side wall was a door; the one on the right led along a small passage to a bedroom at the end, with on the left of the passage, a cloakroom with toilet and basin. On the other side of the main room the door led into another passage with a full bathroom complete with bidet on the right, a smaller bedroom on the left with a sliding window and at the end the main bedroom with double sliding doors onto the terrace. The whole flat had an open airy feel to it and the view beyond the louvred shutters overlooked the fort. The floors of course were all tiled.

However, this was not all. We were ushered outside and through the main door into the tiled entrance hall and into the lift. There were five floors and after alighting at the top one we climbed another set of stairs and out onto an open terrace running the whole length of the roof with magnificent views along the coast. In the centre of the roof a row of laundries had been built, all with their own lockable doors, and the one for the flat we were looking at was right at the far end. Inside, the room was a good size with a sink and a door leading out on the other side to an open drying area separated from the one next door by a wire-netting fence. In addition, in the underground garage there was a parking space for a car.

The price for all this was 11 million pesetas which, at the current and ever-fluctuating exchange rate was in the region of £20,000. We then sat down with the owner and Clara for a bit of serious bargaining, all conducted in Spanish of course, of which we understood not a word. Now and again Clara would break off to translate a little of the proceedings. Having established that the price was acceptable, it was then to be arranged as to how payment would be made. The first thing we had to understand was the Spanish way of registering the price of any house or flat. In essence, the actual selling price was not the one to be registered with the tax authorities. A lower price would be established at a well-recognised level and put forward as the price paid, and this was the one which would be subject to the tax levied on the sale, much as we would pay stamp duty, but probably a bit more complicated. The full asking price, in our case, would be paid in three instalments starting with a deposit of £5,000,

172

or the equivalent in pesetas. We promised to arrange this on our return to the UK and took the builder's bank details in order to make the transfer.

Meanwhile he would move his office to the flat on the other side and have the walls painted white in our flat. We had turned down this other flat despite it having two full bathrooms as it was quite a bit more expensive, as were some of the flats for sale on the upper floors where the view was better. As this would only be a holiday flat, it did not seem practical to pay the extra for another bathroom which we would rarely use.

The furnishing and the kitchen installation would have to wait until later, but eventually we were able to buy all we needed in the big display rooms on the Poligano, as the industrial area was known. Unlike the UK where the time between order and delivery could be anything up to two months, whatever we chose was delivered the next day.

The curtain shop at the top of the road not only came and measured all our windows, they also made all the curtains, brought all the fittings and put them up for us. In Spanish fashion, once we had placed the order the shop owner took us all out for coffee and a brandy in the café next door. I really liked doing business in Spain!

Alex always left our finances to me, and although I had no very clear idea of how I would find the money for the flat, I had no doubt that it would be possible. I planned to take out a bank loan for £5,000 to pay the deposit and after that I would have to think of a way to raise the next £10,000. However, luck was on our side. We returned home from our holiday to find the usual pile of mail behind the front door, and as I sorted it all out I could hardly believe it when I found a letter from my tenant in the downstairs flat in Chillingham Road. She was getting married, she said, and would be moving into her new husband's home and therefore was giving me one month's notice on her tenancy! How amazing was that! Mrs Robson was still the tenant in the upstairs flat where her controlled rent was minimal. I had to apply to the Rent Board every other year to increase it in line with current inflation.

So it was with great delight that I wrote giving my congratulations and wishing my tenant all the best in her new life, while at the same time contacting the local estate agent and putting the flat on the market for £15,000. In the course of time we got a buyer, but as this was a second home I had to pay capital gains tax, as well as the estate agent's fees, but eventually I was able to send £10,000 to Spain and also pay for the furnishings and kitchen.

Meanwhile, our trips to Majorca were sheer pleasure as we revelled in having our own home there. We enjoyed going early in the year while the island was still quiet. We had fitted cupboards put up in the laundry, as well as the washing machine, and we kept folding chairs up there and would sit out in the drying area catching the winter sun. I had now spent much the same amount of time in England as I had spent in South Africa, 15 years in each case. When first I arrived back in England with my children and our few possessions, I could never have imagined that one day all this would have happened to us.

Over the next year or so I felt my health was failing although I did not know what the cause was. I became prone to terrible chest infections which left me with bronchitis, often lasting for weeks before my chest cleared again. I continually suffered from painful sinusitis with accompanying headaches which lasted for weeks rather than days. My joints would ache and my scalp became coated with thick dandruff, while my eyelids were inflamed and encrusted. Sometimes the side of my face and my jaw ached, although a visit to the dentist found nothing wrong with my teeth.

Whenever I went to my GP about my chest infections, the first question I was always asked was whether or not I smoked. As soon as I said I had never been a smoker, it became obvious that that was the end of the matter and there was no other solution on offer. So concerned were they at work that it was arranged for me to go to a Harley Street specialist to have sensitivity tests done on my skin, but I was not allergic to any of the pollens and dusts with which I was tested.

I remember one day as I walked alongside the tennis courts to make a visit to Coram Fields, my coughing fit was so bad that I sank to the ground in order to catch my breath. At home I would fall asleep in front of the television every night and could barely bring myself to have a conversation with anyone because of the thumping headaches which clouded everything I said and did. I would catch the train into Victoria Station in the early morning, and sometimes it took all my willpower to prevent myself getting straight back on and going home. Something was definitely wrong, but I had no idea what.

One day my daughter Anne brought me some women's magazines she had finished reading and in one of them I found an article entitled 'Not all in the Mind'. It was a review of a book with that title just published by a doctor, whose name to my regret I can no longer recall. In the book he wrote of many patients he had treated who had been at the end of their tether due to symptoms remarkably like mine, having been brushed off by various doctors as being hypochondriacs who were imagining all these wildly differing symptoms which did not add up to any recognisable disease. As I read, it was though a light had shone through at last. At the end of the article, a list of symptoms was printed, with the advice that anyone suffering from five or six of them, was probably suffering from food sensitivity ... I had most of them. Food sensitivity! Could that be at the root of all my problems?

175

I could hardly wait to buy the book and read it avidly. The author suggested that the only way to see if food sensitivity was the problem was to clear out the system with a basic diet of things that were known to be harmless, and then to gradually add back into the diet the things that could possibly be harmful.

As a basic diet he advised plain boiled rice, pears, evaporated milk and stewed minced veal. Fortunately the wonderful butcher down in Soho could provide the minced veal while the Berwick Street market sold all the pears I could want. All the other items were readily available. To be successful, I would have to keep not only a strict record of all that I ate in diary form, but also a record of any results from this diet. So on day one I had a breakfast of boiled rice with evaporated milk and a cup of hot water. For lunch I took to work some boiled rice and three ripe pears. Dinner at home was half a pound of veal mince, some rice, two pears, and a cup of hot water and evaporated milk.

By the end of the day, my throat was sore, my joints all ached, I had an intense headache and I could hardly lift up my head through drowsiness. As advised I took a teaspoon of bicarbonate in a glass of warm water and found immediate relief. If I had ever thought this was never going to work, my experience on that first day made me realise that I was probably on to a solution to all my problems.

After three days I began to add in other foods as recommended in the book, first a banana. Then cornflakes and a helping of shepherd's pie when we all went out to lunch at work one day. But at the end of the fourth day I suddenly had the most extreme diarrhoea, thankfully while I was at home and not at work. There could be no doubt that my body was responding, and responding violently to the withdrawal of so many things which had obviously been presenting my digestive system with more than it could cope with. I even discovered that an eye cream I had been using caused my eyes to become inflamed and sore.

176

After about three weeks I had a list of foods to which I reacted, which included chicken or any poultry, nuts, grapefruit, cheese, All Bran or wholemeal of any kind, and tea and instant coffee. Almost overnight my whole life changed. I still remember walking down towards Kings Cross station one morning, when suddenly my sinuses cleared and for the first time in many months I could breathe. My headaches went, and all the aches and pains, my scalp cleared, as did the depression, the neuralgia and the recurrent bronchitis.

I felt as though I was walking on air. I shall be forever thankful to that doctor who discovered the problem and took the trouble to write about it. It would be nice to think that someone may read this account of mine and recognise the problem that they have, for only recently I have read articles by doctors denying that such things as food sensitivities exist. Well, I have news for them!

Meanwhile, I realised that the volume of work coming through our office was beginning to decrease as employers got to grips with the system. There was a brief flurry of extra work as the statutory sick pay scheme got under way and we had to visit employers with a big payroll and explain the new system to them. As I had thought while in Sunderland, it had been decided that the payment of Sickness Benefit by the Department was too labour intensive, and now it was all handed over to employers to administer, claiming the payments of benefit back from the Government. But as this too became better understood, I could see that before long this office in Soho would eventually be run down and probably closed. It was time to look ahead and make some decisions, so I was happy to be put forward for the HEO promotion boards and was selected to go for an interview for a post at the Export Credit Guarantee Board, a scheme which gave assistance to companies exporting goods abroad.

The interview was to take place in Cardiff, so I caught the train there and took a taxi to the very prestigious headquarters. On the way there, the taxi driver held forth at length on the glories of Welsh rugby, all the while turning to talk to me as he asserted that there was a quarry in the Welsh hills where all good rugby players were hewed. Anxious to arrive in one piece I agreed with all he said in the vain hope that he would keep his attention on the road, but I can only assume that he had eyes in the back of his head, as we arrived at our destination in perfect safety.

The offices themselves were mostly open plan with not a window in view, and as I chatted to the receptionist she told me that no one liked working in the place. Eventually I was called into a room where four men were seated behind a desk and was asked to take a seat facing them. The interview went well as I had read up on their activities beforehand and was able to show I knew how they functioned.

In addition I had been talking to the husband of a friend of mine who was the accountant for a large company. When I had told him of my impending interview, he told me that from time to time his company sent quite sizeable cheques to the Export Credit Guarantee Board and they were astonished at how long it took them to present them to the bank for payment. During the interview I told them what I had heard, and they looked a bit startled and gave each other some long looks. Whatever the reaction to my comments had been, some days later I was told that I had passed the board and would soon be notified as to when I could start at their offices in London. But before that could happen, the whole edifice of the Export Credit Guarantee scheme came tumbling down as it came to light that companies in some countries, notably Nigeria and Poland, had been defrauding the scheme on a massive scale. The whole thing was closed down. Somewhat chastened, I carried on as usual and as an afterthought put in a request to work at our headquarters, although I wasn't all that keen on doing that.

The following week we flew to Majorca for a couple of weeks, taking with us our deposit of £5,000 for our apartment. At last we were given the keys and went to see the place again, revelling in its spaciousness and charm. Paul and Clara introduced us to the man who had installed the kitchen in their flat when they bought it. He had business premises on the industrial site outside Palma where, taking the kitchen measurements with us, we were able to go and choose the kitchen units and show him how we would like them to be set out, leaving space for a large fridge/freezer.

Although my three older children, Anne, Paul and Christopher, were happily married and settled down, Cathleen had been a source of concern for us for some time. Unknown to us, she had been suffering from a mild form of epilepsy for some years which manifested itself in occasional lapses of concentration that had gone unnoticed by anyone, probably due to her general learning difficulties. However, when it was time for her to leave school at 16, a few years after we had moved to Croydon, a job was found for her in a small local factory which she settled into very well to begin with. But then it was discovered that, when she was under any sort of stress, she would have a full-scale epileptic seizure and the problem finally came to light. Often I would be contacted at work from any of the south London hospitals where she might have been admitted.

Different jobs were found for her and eventually she went to work at a research facility in Shirley which was attached to the Maudsley Hospital on Denmark Hill. Thus it was that whenever she had an especially severe seizure, that was where they sent her. They did many tests and eventually she was given a place in a residential centre attached to the hospital where we were able to visit her on a regular basis. As she improved, a place was found for her at the David

Lewis Centre in Cheshire, a residential set-up for young people suffering from epilepsy.

To begin with newcomers were housed in a pleasant building where there was in-house support, but with time, and as they improved, they would be moved to more self-sufficient units and taught how to look after themselves. Once well enough, they took part in various activities around the grounds such as woodwork and farming for the boys and housework and creative activities for the girls. The various units were laid out in spacious grounds with the buildings looking like small Tudor cottages. We were thankful that Cathleen was being well cared for and gradually learning how to make her way in the world and we had high hopes that eventually she would be able to return home and live a fulfilled life.

16

We had decided right from the start that we would not turn our flat into a holiday let, but we were happy for friends and relations to have the use of it. So every year our elder daughter Anne would spend the month of August there with her three children, her husband joining her for the final two weeks.

Over the years there were other visitors. My auntie May and her son David, my sister-in-law Margery from South Africa, and later a friend called Joyce, who spent her honeymoon there with her husband Ray; all travelled over and had the use of the flat. Alex's sister Irene and her husband Dave joined us one year for a two-week break and on another occasion our friends Ted and Betty stayed with us too.

For ourselves, we revelled in our holidays there, exploring the island where we discovered beautiful beaches along the undeveloped eastern coast, while in the town of Manacor where the pearl factory was, we bought well-made pieces of occasional furniture for the flat at the local shops. As there was no English TV, of course, we made our own amusements and out on the terrace we had a table where a large jigsaw was in place. We also played Scrabble and for entertainment we bought a tape recorder and built up a good stock of our favourite music. As we were both avid readers, we would buy a selection of the latest paperbacks on our way through the airport, and then at an exchange shop in El Arenal we would sell those we had read and buy another selection.

A new road was built around the fort making a short cut around the back of the village, and trees were planted across the vacant ground. It made for an easier walk to the area beyond the fort and we would go for lunch at one of the many small cafés around there. One of our favourites was in a courtyard where a barbecue was set up in one corner. It was overseen by a swarthy man in a large white apron who, all the time he was flipping over the roasting meat, would have a cigarette hanging from the corner of his lip. As he rarely took it out of his mouth, it was anyone's guess where the ash fell. But all these things were in the future. In the spring of 1985, our thoughts began to turn to the coming years as we were within striking distance of retirement, or certainly near enough to start to map out some plans.

So we decided that once we had both retired we would spend our winters in Majorca and our summers in the UK. The obvious solution was to sell the house in Shirley, buy a two-bedroomed flat and look for a place in the country. So we put the house on the market and it was sold to a lovely Indian couple who were the first people to come and view it. Prices had begun to rise, even then, and we sold it for £65,000. We hunted high and low for a reasonably sized flat, and had almost despaired of finding anything when we went to view a two-bedroomed flat in a suburb of Croydon called Woodside. On a large well-kept site there were two identical blocks of flats, each flat having its own garage in a separate block.

The one we viewed was on the second floor, where a carpeted landing contained the front doors to two flats and floor to ceiling windows let in loads of light. The front door to the flat we viewed led into a passage running down to the door of the lounge/dining room at the end where the large room filled the width of the flat. Back at the front door and off the passage to the left was an airing cupboard, then the bathroom, then the well-fitted kitchen, while on the right was the smaller bedroom and next to it the larger, both with built-in cupboards. The young couple who were selling it were moving further out of the London area with their young baby. The price was £33,000 so we put in an offer of £32,500 which was accepted.

The next task was to look for a place somewhere in the Kent countryside, a wooden chalet or bungalow perhaps, nothing very sophisticated. The best place to look for something like that was the *Exchange and Mart* magazine, as such sales would have to be on a cash basis and would hardly feature in the window of the local estate agent. Finally we found a wooden chalet advertised near a place called Meopham in Kent, so we phoned the number, made an appointment for the weekend and wrote down the directions.

It was with great excitement that we drove out there that Saturday. We had to turn off the main road and drive along a narrow winding country lane lined by large, individually designed homes until we reached a turning onto a dirt road on the left called Rhododendron Avenue. Immediately I was entranced. We passed tiny wooden buildings, some not more than shacks, some looking deserted, while others gleamed with fresh paint. The track was rutted and needed careful driving as we began to descend into a wooded valley, passing one after the other of these individually built homes, each set in a substantial piece of ground.

Further and further we went while the ground rose up on our left and on our right, until at last we reached the one we were looking for. We pulled into the driveway and stepped out of the car into the peace of that lovely valley, and soon were greeted by the occupants of the little wooden shack we had come to see. After we had been shown around, they told us the history of this little hideaway valley, which neither then nor later were we able to verify. According to them the whole valley was known as Happy Valley and had been owned by a newspaper magnate whose heirs had divided it up into half- or quarter-acre plots which were sold freehold. Between the two world wars many of these little homes had

183

been built to house the hop-pickers who came down every summer, so that as far as the local authorities were concerned, residence could only be for nine months of the year. As our plan was to live in Majorca during the winter this did not worry us, although we were told that many people, including the sellers, had lived here permanently for many years, with the council turning a blind eye. Others, of course, used them as holiday homes and many had owned them for a number of years.

Price was discussed and we made an offer which they said they would consider. We left, but a week or so later we were sad to receive a phone call to say they had accepted a higher offer. We were so in love with the area, however, that we were not willing to give up easily, so one day we drove back to the row of shops in the village, and put an advertisement in the paper shop window saying we were looking for a place to buy in Rhododendron Avenue. We hoped we might be lucky, but only time would tell. I was thankful that I had regained my good health as the complications of dealing with all these transactions, as well as a full time job, could have been very stressful.

Shortly after we moved into the flat, our little corgi Bobby became ill. He began to lose the use of his hind legs and became incontinent. It soon became apparent that he was in great distress as his kidneys had begun to fail and so, reluctantly, we had him put to sleep. As we drove to the vets, I held him on my knee and he seemed to sense that all was not well as he shivered and snuggled under my arm. We returned home without him and for several days, I woke up weeping. I had so many happy memories of that little dog. There was the occasion when I was sitting in our garden on a low chair when suddenly the Red Arrows flew over during a display they were giving at Biggin Hill. Startled by the sudden noise, Bobby leapt onto my knee and we both went flying over backwards. Not forgetting his love of a good roll on the thick rug in the hall resulting in a layer of dog hairs on it. It was as though we had lost a child and we decided that there would be no more animals.

One day we had a phone call from the David Lewis Centre to say that Cathleen had been admitted to intensive care at the Macclesfield Hospital, so we packed an overnight bag and set off to drive to Cheshire. It was dark by the time we arrived at the hospital and were directed to the intensive care ward where Cathleen lay unconscious. The doctor came to see us and explained that she had had a series of seizures and that they had had to give her heavy doses of medication to halt them. He said that, as she had been given the maximum doses, should they not work and the seizures start up again, there would be nothing they could do and she would be unlikely to survive the strain.

We were directed to the relatives' room with the assurance that they would call us if there was any change. There was a pay phone there and we called Anne and gave her the news, then settled down as best we could on the leather loungers that were provided in the room. The night went slowly but thankfully we were not called, and early next morning we went back to the ward where we found that Cathleen had regained consciousness but was now in a deep sleep.

We drove to the David Lewis Centre to tell them the news and to ask if they knew of somewhere local where we could stay for a few days. They very kindly offered us the use of a flat in a disused building where at one time a resident doctor had been housed before finances had dried up. It was on the top floor of an otherwise empty building and, while being very spartan, it provided all we could need and we were most grateful. On the staircase coming up there was a pay phone which would also accept calls, which the hospital phone had not, and we phoned Anne to report back. She told us that Paul was flying over that afternoon and gave us the flight number and time of arrival of his plane at Manchester Airport.

We returned to the hospital, where Cathleen was still very drowsy, before driving to the airport to pick up Paul. We took him straight to the hospital where Cathleen was at last able to say a few words although she found it hard to understand what Paul was doing there. Fortunately the flat had two bedrooms so we were able to put Paul up as well, and as there was a kitchen we bought the makings for sandwiches and breakfast items. By the next day Cathleen was much better, so we drove Paul back to the airport where, with his Dan Air connections, he was able to get a seat on a plane returning to Majorca. After another day when Cathleen was well on the way to recovery, we finally left and drove back home.

A few days later we had a phone call from a gentleman who had seen our advert in the shop at Meopham. He had a chalet he wished to sell and wanted to know if we were still interested. We certainly were, so we arranged to go down there again the next weekend.

Once more we drove along the country lane, but as we had been instructed, instead of driving along to the top of Rhododendron Avenue, we turned into another lane called Meadow Lane a few hundred yards before. This shorter rutted and unpaved road eventually joined Rhododendron Avenue at the bottom of the hill, and the place we were coming to see was at the apex on the left-hand side, hidden by a stand of trees. We pulled in behind the car already parked in the parking space beneath the trees from where we could see the long slope of ground to the wooden chalet at the top. As we got out, once more we were impressed by the silence apart from the twittering of the birds and the sound of the wind in the trees. Waiting for us at the top of the slope were the owner and his wife, and we climbed the hill and introduced ourselves.

They explained that they had used the place as a holiday home during the period when their two daughters were growing up, but now they had not bothered with the place for several years so it was in a bit of a dilapidated condition. The outside was clad in greenish-coloured shingles and the front door took a while to open as the wood had swollen. Inside there was a glassed-in passage onto which an inner window opened. Through another door at the end was a living room with a kitchen behind it that obviously needed a great deal of attention. There was a small toilet and a wash basin as well as a small bedroom. Dust and cobwebs were everywhere and the curtains at the windows had almost rotted away. However, there was a water supply and sewerage was taken care of by a cess pit, which was not the type that needed to be emptied, but relied on natural processes. There was no electricity, but it was planned to run in a supply from the local grid. All in all the building had little to recommend it but the ground covered a good three-quarters of an acre and the site itself had a commanding position over the valley. A small triangle of level ground was at the back, but otherwise at the front there was nowhere level to sit. Down the fences at either side the hedges were overgrown although the grass in the centre had been cut from time to time and kept in check. We felt that something could be done with it and we finally settled on a price of £14,000. After exchanging the names of our solicitors, we left feeling happy with what we had found.

After Cathleen had recuperated in hospital we travelled back up and brought her home from the David Lewis Centre and settled her into the flat.

Up in Newcastle, Chris and Maggie were expecting their second child and decided to buy a house on a new development in Edenthorpe, just outside Doncaster, Maggie's home town.

187

They barely had time to move into their new home before Lara arrived at Easter in 1986.

We now had eight grandchildren, three of Anne's in London, three of Paul's in Majorca and now two of Chris's in Yorkshire. Keeping up with birthdays was hard work so I let them all know I drew the line at remembering wedding anniversaries!

One day at work my friend Jane asked me if I had noticed the advert in the most recent 'D' circular for an HEO to work in the Fees Office at the House of Commons to, as it said, 'assist MPs to be better employers'. I had glanced at it but had thought that it would not be for me, but Jane insisted and said that in her opinion I would be tailor-made for the job after my experience with working on the benefit system, as well as on National Insurance. So, not entirely convinced, I sent off for the application form after informing our manager of what I was doing. He gave me his full support which encouraged me to send the completed form off to the House of Commons.

Before long I received an invitation on House of Commons headed notepaper to go for an interview by a Selection Board at 3 Dean's Yard adjacent to the west door of Westminster Abbey on March 26th 1986 at 10.45 am.

Suitably dressed, I arrived far too early so took the opportunity to go and sit in the peaceful surroundings at the rear of the Abbey to quieten my nerves. Eventually I approached the flight of steps leading to the door of 3 Dean's Yard and a man at the reception desk asked me to wait as he phoned for someone to come and get me. I was escorted upstairs and once again was asked to wait in the personnel office. Feeling uncomfortable, and being largely ignored by the staff working there, I was glad when at last I was called into the room where I was to be interviewed.

Three men and a lady sat behind the regulation interviewing desks and as I sat down facing them my nerves calmed and I felt quite relaxed. As the questioning began, they were interested in what I had done to date, as well as in the job with which I was currently involved. I also told them of the fiasco with the Export Credit Guarantee Board which they apparently had never heard about. I had taken the trouble to read up on some of the unemployment law which I had never previously been involved with, so was able to give a comprehensive description of what a case of constructive dismissal would involve.

All in all I came away feeling that I had done as well as I could and having done my best, the result was in the lap of the gods. As I passed through the entrance hall on my way out, a very large lady dressed a bit like an unmade bed was waiting to go for her interview. Poor soul, I thought, she looked so terribly nervous.

The following week we were due to fly to Majorca for a couple of weeks taking with us the final payment for the flat. Due to the favourable exchange rate at the time, we only needed another £3,200 to complete the deal, as well as the legal fees. As the result of my interview would probably come through during our time there, our manager asked me to leave Paul's phone number with him, promising to let me know as soon as he heard, as the information would come through to him first.

Once back in Majorca we happily took possession of the keys to the flat and began the search for furniture and curtains, at the same time arranging for the installation of the kitchen. A few days before we were due to return, a phone call came from my boss in England. I had got the job at the House of Commons and once I was back home, dates would be arranged for me to leave the civil service and become a Crown Servant instead.

17

I remember once hearing Barry Humphreys in his persona as Dame Edna Everidge talking about the criteria of name dropping. As he said, 'You may know *them*, but do they know *you!*' Over the next few years I was to know many of *them*, but few, if any, were very aware of *me*. So if I name any names, it is with that thought in mind. I was there to do a job and was merely one of the underlings. For all that, the next four years were filled with interest.

On my first day I was taken from our office in Dean's Yard over to the House of Commons, and furnished with a security pass which would allow me access to the main building without having to go through the stringent security checks set up after the tragic death of Airey Neave in a car bomb attack.

I was then introduced to the HEO from whom I was taking over on his retirement. Almost his first sentence to me was that I would be dealing with 'six hundred and fifty megalomaniacs most of whom are thugs'. That sentence put things into perspective for me, not because of the 'megalomaniacs', nor even because of the 'thugs' but because of the six hundred and fifty people I would be dealing with. *Six hundred and fifty!*

I would challenge anyone to sit down and try to list as many MPs as possible. I would say it would take a genius to come up with a hundred names. For most of us, we would do very well to name, say, 25 or 30 ... on a good day and with the wind behind us. So it is true to say that the majority of people I dealt with were quite unknown to me. Not only that, the party they belonged to was rarely known either; our dealings crossed all party lines, as was right and proper that they should.

Our offices in Dean's Yard were old, with creaking floors and few facilities. There was nowhere for the staff to make tea for instance, and should anyone bring in their own kettle etc., water was available from a tap above a huge white Belfast sink set in the corridor outside the office I shared with another HEO. The section I was to be in charge of was on the first floor in a large room facing into Dean's Yard. I and my colleague, Ben, were in a small room on the next floor on the other side of the building facing out onto Victoria Street, with windows that were so seldom cleaned that it was hardly possible to see out of them.

The work with which Ben and I were involved was to administer the Office Costs Allowances of the MPs. Ben ran the payroll dealing with the salaries of the MPs secretaries and research assistants, while I dealt with claims for office equipment as well as the Additional Costs Allowance, a tax-free sum to enable MP's to fund a second home, either in London or in their constituencies. Only those in a designated area adjacent to the House of Commons were debarred from claiming.

From day one my biggest problem was that there was no rule book. Having spent so many years working to an exact set of rules meticulously set out in 'Codes', as the books of rules were called, I found that here nothing was written down and all I was told was that I should remember that I was dealing with 'honourable gentlemen'. My boss, whose designation was 'Accountant' although as far as I knew neither he nor his compatriots at that level had probably ever taken any accountancy exams, was less than helpful and his answers to my queries were so vague that I soon gave up asking for any advice, realising that I was on my own.

The allowances ran from April to March in line with the

191

tax year, and as the end of the tax year approached I would be bombarded with requests for a forecast of the amount of money that would be left over after the staff salaries had been taken into account up to end of the tax year. This I was quite happy to do, as although a computer had been installed at great expense it was only capable of producing a payroll and was quite unable to add in the torrent of day-to-day claims for other office costs which had to be run separately.

In effect, we administered a payroll on behalf of 650 employers who employed, at the most two or maybe three people, many of them never having employed anyone before, which was where I came in. There was also a pension scheme for the MPs' staff which I was not involved with.

One drawback to this new job was that I no longer had the benefit of flexi-time. My hours were set from 10 am to 6 pm while Ben started at 9 and finished at 5, the idea being that there was an overlap just in case any of the folk in the 'Big House' needed an answer to a query. The large offices overlooking Dean's Yard on our floor were for the use of the accountants, but strangely they were seldom to be found at their desks. While the House was sitting, on a Friday we all waited impatiently for the bell sounding the end of business at around 2.30 pm when we were all at liberty to join the stampede to the doors. If the session overran, for any reason, we could not go until the bell went.

However, these were all minor irritations set against the thrill of entry to one of our greatest institutions. I recalled the day in 1970 when, filling in time on our way to Gatwick to enjoy one of the early package holidays, I had queued with my family to enter the House and to sit in the visitors' gallery of the Chamber of the House of Commons. Never in my wildest imagination did I ever think I would be working there so many years down the line.

While the site on which the building stands has been in use since Roman times, the building itself dates from the

1830s after a fire in 1834 destroyed all but St Stephen's Chapel and the Great Westminster Hall, although the latter was badly damaged. Following on a competition for the best design, won by Charles Barry, the rebuilding took more than 15 years to complete. In 1941 the Chamber of the House of Commons was destroyed by enemy bombs and the MPs were unable to return to their restored chamber until October 1950.

Inside the place is a veritable warren of passages and unexpected staircases where one could visualise the White Rabbit from Alice in Wonderland suddenly appearing. I never ceased to feel a thrill as I walked up the entrance stairs, passing Westminster Hall on the left and then on through St Stephen's Chapel and into the great central lobby.

On one occasion I was able to arrange for a party of us to be given a tour of the Clock Tower which houses 'Big Ben' the enormous bell which chimes out the hours and quarter hours. It is linked electronically to the Greenwich Observatory so that twice a day its performance is checked for accuracy. We climbed the steep stairs to a room below the workings of the clock where, we were told, a suffragette was once locked up by the Sergeant-at-Arms for several days after she had chained herself to the railings of the House. Above, it was awesome to see the massive workings of the clock and to stand inside the famous face. The great pendulum hangs in a chamber made of cast iron to protect it from the wind, which on the day I visited was whistling through the apertures. One interesting fact we were given was that the chimes of Big Ben were written by Handel and set to the following lines:

All through this hour, Lord be my Guide.
And by thy power, no foot shall slide.

Hardly the greatest of poetry, but who could argue with the sentiments.

Back in the House, on the floor below the Chamber were many rooms with various purposes. There were several restaurants catering for staff, quite a few well-patronised bars and outside, facing the Thames, the famous terrace. As a lowly HEO I was not allowed access to this, but during the summer when the House was not sitting, a blind eye was turned and on a fine day I would take a book and my sandwiches and enjoy the sun streaming in from its south-facing aspect.

Along that frontage were several Members' Dining Rooms which could be hired for special events and I was fortunate to be invited by the Secretaries and Assistants Council to a champagne and strawberry tea where the well-respected Betty Boothroyd was also a guest.

Occasionally other invitations came my way, and not long after I started at the Fees Office I attended a visit by the President of the Federal Republic of Germany. As is always the case, the event was meticulously timed and arranged, and before going I received a copy of the programme with minute-by-minute instructions, from the arrival at the Royal Gallery of Peers, of Members of Parliament at the Prince's Chamber, and guests and press (us) at the Norman Porch. Accompanied by a fanfare of trumpets the president was led to the dais by the Lord Great Chamberlain, the Rt. Hon. the Lord Hailsham of St Marylebone and the Speaker, the Rt. Hon. Bernard Weatherill. Also present were Margaret Thatcher, Willie Whitelaw and John Biffin. Quite an occasion. I have often been asked if I ever met Margaret Thatcher and the answer is no. I was not that far up the hierarchy, but I did correspond with her over an increase in her secretary's salary.

In July of 1986 some of us were given tickets to stand on the pavement of the east side of Parliament to watch the wedding procession of Prince Andrew and Sarah Ferguson and we all cheered as the bride swept past, and even more so on the return journey as they both grinned and waved wildly. It was obvious that Sarah was enjoying every moment!

The Fees Office was so named because, when it was set up long ago, Members made very modest claims for expenses as they mostly had other income and served in Parliament as a public duty. Over the years things have changed, but the name stuck. However, a culture of strict adherence to unspoken rules pervades the whole of Parliament, and to a stranger there is a great sense of awe and dignity about the place. A story is told of a group of American visitors who were being escorted on a tour of the House. Suitably subdued and impressed they were being led along an echoing corridor when a Member rushed past them trying to catch up with Sir Neil MacFarlane with whom he wanted a word. In his haste he shouted at the top of his voice, 'Neil!' and, so the story goes, all the American visitors dropped to their knees.

The pomp and circumstance of the place is best revealed by the Speaker's procession. Each day that the House sits, the Speaker's procession goes from the robing room through the great central lobby where the Sergeant-at-Arms calls out 'Hats off strangers!' With great dignity, and in silence, they make their way to the right and through to the Commons where the Speaker takes his seat on the beautifully carved Speaker's chair.

In June of 1987, the year after I joined the Fees Office, there was a General Election where the Conservative government held on to power, but the chaos that ensued in our office had to be seen to be believed. The moment the results began to come through all work on the secretarial pay had to cease and the accountants were kept on their toes as the successful candidates were listed in the media. For those who retained their seats all went well, but for those who lost, that usually meant a change of party and their loyal staff would generally leave with them, as the new incumbent would have staff of his or her own choosing.

The section that paid Members their salaries and car expenses were equally affected, but for the secretaries, many of whom made a career of working in the House, there would be a great scramble to find another post. The 'new' boys and girls were interviewed by the accountants and were signed up for their salaries and told what they could claim for their staff and expenses. For my part I took on the task of working out redundancy payments for secretaries who had lost their position, and at the same time administering the allowance for MPs who had lost their seat, a set sum to help them to clear up their parliamentary affairs. Ben, meanwhile, was kept busy with P60s for the leavers and personal details for new staff.

Among those newly elected was David Blunkett who, because of his disability, was awarded a much greater Office Costs Allowance to help him to employ readers and extra staff to cope with his day-to-day affairs. So from time to time I would go over to his office in the House to set out for him the details of his very complicated affairs. His guide dog at the time was called Offa, from whom I would receive a slobbery welcome which, being a dog lover, I took in my stride. We would then go over all the salaries he was paying including the factored-in payment of employer's National Insurance, and also list all that had been spent on various pieces of office equipment. It never ceased to amaze me that he had all the details at his fingertips. Truly an awesome mind.

Another newcomer that year was Dr Marjorie Mowlam from Redcar, or 'Mo' as she was affectionately known. She would sweep into our office, pull out a chair and put her feet up on the desk all the while regaling us with hilarious chit-chat. What a woman.

Also a great favourite was John Prescott who would chat

for a while on a one-to-one basis, making jokes about 'her indoors' and on one famous occasion came into the office with a cheque for £5,000 to keep his allowance in balance. At the time he was extremely busy as Shadow Transport Minister as there had been train crashes at Clapham and Purley as well as a pile-up on the M6 at Sandbach.

My own personal favourite was Frank Field who had been an MP for a few years, always calm and gentlemanly, courteous with a well-modulated voice. Unlike some, whose names I will not mention but who were generally disliked for their aggression and rudeness to the staff generally.

One day Stuart Bell, the Member for Middlesbrough, came in. At the time there had been a terrible scandal concerning child abuse in his constituency. As a good MP will be deeply involved in the concerns of his constituency, Stuart was no exception and he had waded in to support parents wrongly accused of abusing their children during 1987. We had a long discussion about the case and he told me much that had not been publicised. Two doctors had, on the basis of an anal test, had 197 Cleveland children taken into care on extremely flimsy grounds. The case became a national *cause célèbre* and to Stuart's thinking it equated with the Salem Witch Hunts in America in 1692. His well-researched book on the case, *When Salem Came to the Boro*, was published and later on he very kindly sent me a signed copy. A splendid example of what a good MP can do.

Of course, as ever, the House was not free from the occasional scandal, as an event in March 1989 was to prove. It was alleged that a research assistant employed by an MP made £500 a night as a high-class call girl. Unwittingly, I became involved when I received a phone call from a journalist asking if MPs were entitled to employ whoever they wished as an assistant. I confirmed that they could, but was appalled the following day to be quoted in the *Guardian* as having said that they could 'claim the allowance without hiring anyone and instead farm out the odd bit of typing to a local secretarial agency'. A patent lie as such an action would not have been possible. After that though, I never answered any queries from the press, and referred them to a higher authority.

Administering the allowances was not always plain sailing. With no rules to be guided by, I often had to use my common sense and fortunately the EO in charge of the allowance section, through whose hands the bulk of the claims came, would pull out the most excessive for me to have a look at. So when, for instance, a claim came in for a large amount for 'building and repairs', it was possible for me to send a very diplomatic letter asking in the most polite of terms for the relevant invoices and receipts 'so that payment may be made without delay'. When nothing more was heard, the claim would be quietly dropped. In other cases a letter from me would go out stating that 'during a recent audit, it was discovered that...' As no audits ever took place this was a bit of chicanery, but on the other hand, more often than not it resulted in the claims being withdrawn.

I was on firmer ground when it came to employment of staff. Attempts to have a secretary or researcher treated as 'self-employed' or for cash lump sums to be given for 'casual work' could be resisted as there are hard and fast laws laid down in these cases. It was never easy to come between an MP and his or her money however, and I had more than one irate Member on the phone telling me in no uncertain terms that '... it's *my* money' when in fact it was the taxpayers' money he or she was spending.

That October I was given a pass to the State Opening of Parliament, an occasion I shall never forget. We all had to be in place an hour before the Queen was due to arrive and we stood on wooden tiers set along both sides of the Royal Gallery which leads from the Robing Room through to the House of Lords. TV screens were set along the walls so that we could see all that was happening outside, which made

198

the long stand bearable. On them we could see the first coach to arrive containing the Imperial Crown, after which the Queen arrived. She was robed and put on the Crown in the privacy of the Robing Room. Her procession then went along the Royal Gallery. I was fairly near the front with a good view of the Queen, the Duke of Edinburgh and Princesses Margaret and Alexandra as they slowly made their way to the House of Lords. We remained where we were for the whole of the ensuing ceremony, watching all the proceedings on the TV screens, until at last the procession returned to the Robing Room and we were able to leave. My one moan was that I had to wear a hat! Something I hate.

There was to be one more big occasion shortly before I retired. I was given tickets for Alex and myself to attend the Queen's Birthday Parade on the June 16th 1990, better known as The Trooping of the Colour. Starting at 11 am we had to be in our places on the stands along the edges of Horse Guards Parade in good time. As ever, the arrangements were impeccable and the timing spot on and, being fortunate with the weather, we revelled in such a very British occasion.

18

Shortly before I began work at the House of Commons we finally took possession of the chalet at Meopham. There had been some unaccountable delay on the part of our sellers, but as the money was tucked up in a nice high-earning savings account, we came out with more money than we had started with. This went a long way to pay to have a proper electrical cable run between ourselves and a small place next door, with whom we were able to share the costs.

We were also fortunate in the water supply to our place as we were the last in a row of chalets running along the top of the slope, the one at the other end being adjacent to Whitepost Lane where all the individually designed executive houses were. It seemed that, during the war, this part of the valley was used to house soldiers in a temporary camp with a rifle range where, deep in the Kent countryside, they could get to grips with their training. Consequently, a water supply had been run all along the top of the slope and was connected to the main grid. Further down Rhododendron Avenue they were not so lucky and water was brought in from a stand pipe under a somewhat makeshift system which did not always work.

With vital water and electricity supply sorted, the next job was to redesign the jumbled interior. Alex had taken retirement from the Post Office so was able to spend more time on the site. Still living in our comfortable flat, I would set off for work each day and Alex would drive to Meopham. At the weekends we camped out in the available space and worked hard from dawn to dusk. The comparison between this beautiful, serene area and the hustle and bustle, to say nothing of the pomp and circumstance, of the House of Commons was quite striking and I felt as though I was living in two worlds.

We decided that the building would be divided into two. On one side would be an open-plan living/dining and kitchen area, and on the other would be two bedrooms and a shower room cum toilet. So the first task was to demolish all the inner walls which were made of plasterboard fitted to wooden frames, a dusty, dirty task which found us going home on a Sunday evening to the delights of a good shower and hair wash. Alex then fitted fresh frames, one down the centre with a door through to a small lobby, off which would be the shower room at the back and next to it the small bedroom, while at the front was the larger bedroom with a corner window giving magnificent views down the valley and over the tops of the trees. We had stored in our garage at the flat two cream wardrobes from the bedroom suite we had had in the house in Shirley, as our flat was fitted with all the wardrobes we needed. We transported them down to the site and used them as the dividing walls between the two bedrooms, one facing into the back bedroom, and one to the front. The wooden frames to the rooms were clad in sheets of thick plywood made to look like panelling and Alex put large pads of thermal material between the walls to retain the heat.

On the outside we stripped off the ugly felting shingles and were delighted to discover lovely wooden strips which, when treated with preservatives, made the building look like a Swiss chalet.

What was needed more than anything was somewhere to sit outside, so Alex set about building a veranda all along the front. First he put in foundations and built a succession of brick pillars securing the wooden supports on the top. We bought all the planking and I helped him every weekend to gradually make the flooring of our splendid lookout over the valley. I undertook the final job of creosoting all the woodwork as Alex made a firm railing around the edges. He then remade the whole of the front of the building with large windows into the living room and bedroom and a door into each room.

The whole building was transformed from a grotty shed-like and dilapidated shack into a beautiful chalet with a splendid outlook over the valley. In the course of time the kitchen and shower room were completed, the living room carpeted and a pretty built-in cream dressing table put into the bedroom.

One of the first major purchases was a secondhand ride-on mower so that Alex could cope with the wide expanse of grass between the trees at the bottom and the sweep up to the chalet at the top. This area became greatly extended after we had cut back all the hedges lining the sides and burnt the resulting piles of brush. He took great pride in going up and down the slope until, from a distance, it almost resembled a well-kept bowling green!

One summer my granddaughter Adella, Paul's eldest child, came to stay with us for a while. Over the years, every summer when tourism was at its highest pitch Clara, who worked at Palma Airport for a Spanish tourist company, had been in the habit, while her children were small of taking them to stay with her mother in northern Spain. As they grew older, Adella had spent some summers with Anne and her family in England before we had bought the flat in Majorca, since when Anne went there for the summer. Now she was a young teenager, and we were happy to have her come and stay with us for a while.

We took her down to Hastings one day and, after visiting the pirate caves, we went down to see the castle, thinking that she might be interested in our history and culture. After we had roamed around and seen all there was of interest, she casually said to us, 'Of course I've seen all this at Disneyland.' Oh dear, how to distinguish make-believe from reality!

Adella was very keen to try her hand at driving the lawn mower, so one day Alex took it to the flatter area down near the trees and sat her on it, showing her how to work the controls. It suddenly took off while he was still standing near to the machine, and the first I knew of it was when a white-faced Adella came running into the house shouting that Alex had hurt himself. I looked outside to see him limping up the hill. When we got him to sit down and take off his blood-stained shoe, we could see that the cutters of the mower had gone over the toes on one of his feet, leaving most of the end of the big toe in shreds with the bone sticking out. Taking off the sock and wrapping the whole foot in a clean towel, we got him into the car and drove to Casualty at Gravesend Hospital. They told us that they would be unable to treat his injury there, and that we should take him to Dartford Hospital where there were better facilities. At Dartford they decided to admit him and to operate on his foot the next day. Poor Adella was in a terrible state and sobbed uncontrollably, but I comforted her and assured her that it wasn't her fault and that he would be fine. The next day they operated and removed the end of his toe, tucking a flap of skin over the end of it. It soon healed and he was none the worse for his accident.

That winter we had the mower stolen one night as it was not locked up, so of course that meant that we had to buy a new one, but before we did, Alex built a metal shed to house it and keep it locked up when not in use. We also took out insurance! Alex also made a small wooden buggy on wheels to pull behind the mower to use when carrying building materials around the site.

There had not been space to put in a washing machine or provide more storage space, so Alex decided to build on an extension to take care of that, although strictly speaking we were not allowed to extend the living area due to council rules. This became known as Alex's 'bit on the side'. We had been spending more and more time there during the week. I would catch the train to work from Meopham station, so on a Friday Alex would drop me off at the station then drive on to our flat with our laundry, put it all through the washing machine, do the shopping at the local supermarket, and then speed back to pick me up at about 3.30 at Meopham station because of our early Friday finish at the House.

After laying the foundations for the extension, Alex made a prefabricated frame ready to be put into place. The end facing the lane at the bottom was a solid wall of wood strips and in one day he raised the frame and, as he nailed on the outer strips at the front, I stood by with the tin of creosote and painted them to match the rest of the frontage. When it was completed, we installed a long work bench with a washing machine under and a fridge/freezer standing alongside, a good sized wardrobe went into the other end to make enough storage.

Now that we could be self-sufficient down there we decided to sell the flat, as I had a feeling that the property market might be due for a dip in value. Every morning, as Alex drove me to the station at Meopham, we would stop at the local newsagent to pick up the morning paper. At that time, tax relief was given on the interest paid on mortgages under a scheme called Miras, and over the years, as unmarried relationships became more acceptable, such couples had an advantage over a married couple as both partners could claim the Miras tax relief. One morning the newspaper carried an announcement that from the next tax year only one claim for Miras would be allowed on each property. This would also have a big effect on a recent trend in which several young people would buy a large property between them, each one making a claim for the tax relief. This seemed to me to be as good as reason as any to start to think about selling our flat, as it had almost doubled in value. We quickly found a buyer, a young man who had a friend who lived in the other block on the site, and who knew the flats well and was most keen to have one himself. And so we moved permanently into our beautiful little home in the woods. On a fine summer afternoon, Alex would phone me at work as he sat on the veranda drinking a cold beer, making me green with envy as I sat in my stuffy office watching the traffic go by on Victoria Street.

By this time, Cathleen had been helped to establish herself in a flat by a group called the St Katherine's Housing Association, who specialised in helping youngsters with problems such as hers. We were very proud of the progress she had made. She often came down to us for the weekend and enjoyed helping with any work going on. She had got herself a cat, a little female tabby which she brought down with her, but one weekend Alex had just poured a section of concrete for the foundations of the extension when the cat escaped from the house and ran through the lot. We ran to catch her before it began to set and, while she protested in the strongest possible manner, we held her under the outside tap and washed off all the cement. From then on that cat never gave me a kind word or look for the rest of her life.

That was not the last time that Cathleen's cat had an adventure, As we walked up to the chalet one morning, she suddenly came running from behind the house and shinned up a tree, hotly pursued by a young fox. The fox was soon chased off, but it took some persuasion to coax the cat back onto terra firma.

Another pet who did take to us in a big way, however, was Anne's little dog Bonny, a Jack Russell terrier, who came to stay with us for a month in the summer while Anne was at the flat in Majorca with her children. What a little pet she was, always ready for a hug and a game, and from then on, when visiting Anne at home, she would greet us

205

with wild enthusiasm, running up the first few stairs at their home so that she could more easily jump into my arms.

One night, before our flat had been sold, I came back to it after a meeting of our Townswomen's Guild and noticed strangely that the glass doors of our entrance hall were covered in condensation on the outside. The air felt humid and still, although it was the month of October. The next morning, after a peaceful night, I glanced out of our bedroom window and was surprised to see a small flowering tree had been uprooted. When I went to switch on the kettle, we had no electricity. Somewhat puzzled, and unable to access the radio or television, I tried to telephone to report our loss of power, only to find that the telephone was not working either.

There seemed no option but to get ready for work, so we set off in the car for the run down to the station for me to catch my train into London. As we passed the swimming pool, another large tree partly blocked the road, and after skirting it we reached South Norwood station to find the gate that I usually used closed. From others around us, we then learned that there had been a terrible storm during the night and that all the railway lines were blocked by fallen trees. Uncertain what to do next, Alex and I talked it over and decided that I would try to get a bus into town. We drove round to the other side of the station where he dropped me off and I joined the small queue that had formed at the bus stop. After half an hour, when we had all begun to realise that there was very little likelihood of any buses turning up, Alex drove up again, having found out how extensive this storm and its effects had been.

We returned to the flat where we decided that, since there was no chance of me getting into work, we might as well try and drive to Meopham to see what, if any, damage had been done there. It was October 15th 1987, and we were in

206

the aftermath of the worst hurricane ever to hit England.

Packing warm clothing and some sandwiches, we set off to drive through the suburb of West Wickham and were amazed, as we passed the ends of the avenues, to see row after row of trees laid out across the roads, often with cars squashed beneath them. The supermarkets and larger shops were closed, as without electricity they could not operate their tills, while further out into the country whole woods had been stripped of their branches, the tree trunks standing naked like some First World War battlefield. We stopped at a garage for petrol as we were running a bit low, but it was the same story, no electricity so the pumps could not be used.

We decided to make our way to Maidstone to see if there was any better luck there, and on the outskirts found a petrol station that was still functioning. We joined the long queue hoping that their supplies would hold out until we had been served. In true wartime fashion however, they were limiting supplies to about half a tankful, so that more people had the chance to keep moving. The pub next door was also functioning so we stopped long enough to have a hot drink.

Setting off again, we made for Trottiscliffe, the beech-covered hill which wound up towards Meopham and beyond it to Gravesend, but at the roundabout at the bottom of it our way was blocked by dozens of lovely old beech trees all lying jumbled up on the road. It would be many weeks before it was all cleared away. Now that we had some petrol in the tank, we decided to circumvent the area and, pressing on along the M20, we took the A228 up towards Rochester.

Things didn't seem so bad along here, as most of the area was built-up with fewer trees, and soon we were driving towards Gravesend and then back south along the A227 through Meopham village and on to the Whitepost Lane turnoff. As we drove carefully along the lane, we passed one house with a large tree resting drunkenly against it, its branches having punctured the roof. We grimly wondered what we would find down the valley, with its thick coverage of trees and its flimsy wooden chalets. Slowly we turned into Meadow Lane and, approaching our property at the foot of it, facing us we saw exposed the great circular root systems of some of the trees at the bottom of our land. Gracefully draped over them were the tangled remains of the new fencing Alex had just completed. It was obvious that as one tree fell, the others in domino effect had crashed down one after the other. There was no way we could park the car where we normally would have done, and had we been there that night our car would have been a mangled heap of metal by the morning. Hastily we got out and went to our nextdoor neighbour, Joe. He had his daughter staying with him as a few days previously his wife, Violet, had suffered a slight stroke. They told us that all that night they had huddled in terror during the storm, hearing the crashing of the trees around them and wondering if at any moment one would fall and crush their home. Ever the practical one, Joe had rooted out a primus stove and a Kelly lamp, so at least they had light and had been able to make themselves a hot drink and warm up some soup.

Amazingly, no one in the valley suffered either death or injury. One home had caught the brunt of the falling trees and the folk had to be housed elsewhere for a long time while the remains of their chalet were taken down and a new place erected. Another couple had to have a tree dismembered before they were able to use their drive, and the chalet across the road that Joe rented out had a tree propped up against its outer wall. Later when we came to help with the cutting down of that tree, as pieces of the trunk were sawn off, the root system suddenly acted as a fulcrum, and the whole lot tipped back into the hole it had come from.

Our own place was untouched as it was built at the top

of the slope and all the trees were at the bottom. Fortunately we had taken out insurance so Alex was able to claim for his fence, while for weeks afterwards the valley rang to the sound of chainsaws and it was impossible to buy a new one. As we already had one, we were able to pitch in and help with the clearing up until, at length, every property had a big stack of logs waiting for the winter weather.

The next summer we had a visit from my South African nephew Bramwell. His brother Stephen had come to live in England some years before with his South African wife, Louise, and their two boys. While at the David Lewis Centre Cathleen had made an old-fashioned wooden trolley such as boys used to make in the thirties, using pram wheels and a bit of ingenuity. The two front wheels were used to steer with the aid of a rope and they all had great fun trying to ride down the steep slope of the hill without falling off. Alex had a system which kept him firmly on board and was the only one who could reach the bottom without coming a cropper. He had also tied a rope to the branch of one of the trees at the bottom to make a swing and visitors had a lot of fun on that.

19

Cancer. Cancer! Surely not. Within a couple of years of the retirement we were both looking forward to so eagerly, surely it could not be all taken away from us in this way?

Just before we finalised the sale of the flat we were due to go to Majorca for a couple of weeks. I had been reading somewhere that a woman of my age ought to examine her breasts on a regular basis for lumps or any changes so, never having done it before, in the bath one day I ran my hand along the side of my right breast. I thought I could feel a small raised piece, hardly a lump exactly, but just a slightly raised section of no great size. My blood ran cold, could it be possible that the first ever time I checked myself, I had discovered a problem? How bizarre was that. As I had an appointment with my GP for a smear test the week after our return, I decided to leave things until then, as this was to be the occasion of the First Communion of young Pablo. We had already attended the First Communions of the two girls, great occasions for all. The girls would be dressed up like little brides and the boys in white suits, and after the ceremony a hall would be booked with a splendid repast not unlike a wedding reception. This was an occasion not to be missed.

On our return, I duly kept my appointment with the GP and after taking a swab for the smear test, she made a cursory examination of my breasts, failing to notice the raised area on the right one. Tentatively I drew her attention to it, and after pressing and poking at it, obviously somewhat embarrassed, she turned to me and said, 'Oh you clever girl.'

She then pulled out all the stops, trying to get hold of someone at Kings College Hospital as she did not have a very high opinion of May Day, the hospital in Croydon, but to no avail. There was no alternative but to try May Day, although I had no problem with the place myself, and eventually she got an appointment for me later that week. Returning to work, I arranged to take time off without telling anyone why, as there was every possibility that the lump was benign.

On the day of the appointment I was sent for a mammogram to begin with then returned to the clinic where fluid was withdrawn from the lump, an excruciatingly painful experience. I waited while it was tested. There were several other women there and, surprisingly, one man. It seemed that this was a problem not confined to the female sex. Over a cup of tea a lady chatted to us individually if we wished, some sort of counsellor I assumed, and assured us of the great strides that had taken place in the treatment of breast cancer. I could only think of poor Auntie Elsie and the terrible time she had gone through, although my common sense told me that she had neglected going for treatment until her cancer was so well established that really she had no chance.

Eventually I was called into the consultant's office where he sat, a small insignificant-looking little man, behind his outsized desk. He seemed to find it hard to meet my eyes and I could hardly hear him as he mumbled that 'there were some cells there that were a cause for concern' and he would arrange for me to have a lumpectomy. What did that mean? Did I or did I not have cancer? Somewhat dazed I left his room and went to speak to the counsellor lady who was kindness itself, and confirmed what I had suspected, that it was cancer.

Stunned, I returned home to tell Alex, and the next day to inform them at work. They were kindness itself. Our Chief Accountant, Mr J.L.G. Dobson, popularly known as Dobbie, met me in the corridor one morning, and to my astonishment clasped me in his arms and gave me a great bear hug.

I received the letter telling me when to report to the May Day Hospital for my lumpectomy and, packing my little overnight bag, I went with Alex to be admitted.

For some reason they put me into a single room although I would have preferred to have joined other women in a nearby six-bed ward, but I settled myself in and later a young doctor came along to check me out and to explain what would happen the next day. As my lump was small and had been caught early, they would only excise it and part of the breast around it and there would be no need to take away the lymphatic glands under my arm. I began to realise that my spur of the moment examination in the bath had been the best possible thing I could have done.

The next morning I woke early and popped across the corridor to have a quick shower. Before long I had had my pre-meds and was on a trolley joining the queue of other trolleys in the corridor leading to the operating suites. My personal details were checked before I was wheeled into the anti-room to the theatre, a needle was put into the vein on the back of my hand and before I could count up to ten, I knew no more.

Coming to back in my own bed I was aware of a lot of padding on my chest and under my arm. I was visited later by the doctor who said that all had gone well and that I had a drain in from the operation site. I would be referred for radiotherapy which would take place at the Royal Marsden Hospital in Sutton.

A few days later when I had been discharged and the lumpy dressing had been removed, I was able to go back to work as I waited to be given the date for the radiotherapy. Apart from having to go to the doctor's surgery to have the stitches removed – a most painful occasion as they had sunk in quite a lot – I felt quite well and able to function normally.

Finally I had a date for the trip to the Royal Marsden and

we took up residence again down at Meopham, as Alex could more easily drive me around the motorway and onto the access road to Banstead and Sutton. On this first visit I saw the consultant who explained what the procedure would be. He also said that at that time they were conducting some research into the possibility and the effectiveness of having daily radiotherapy, or every other day, or at least twice in one week and three times during the next. If the latter proved to be acceptable, then obviously it would be very cost-effective and in addition it would be less of a hassle for patients who might have to travel long distances. If I were willing to take part, then the choice would be made by a random selection. I said I would be quite happy to take part in this way and I was told that I would be informed as soon as the choice had been made.

A week or so later I was called back to the Marsden and taken to the department where the very accurate measurements were taken to ensure that only the area selected would be bombarded with what could be very dangerous rays. My skin was marked with tattoos at the corners of the site and all the measurements were entered onto a computer disk. I then went to see the consultant again and he told me I had been selected to have the alternate daily treatments which would be on a Monday, Wednesday and Friday one week and a Tuesday and Thursday the next. This suited me fine as it meant I could relax at home for the rest of the time.

The hospital itself was like a comfortable hotel, with armchairs and sofas, a coffee bar and plenty of reading matter. In the radiotherapy suite there were bottles of drinking water and fruit juices to which we could help ourselves as it was advisable to drink plenty of liquids to disperse the effects of the radiotherapy. A positive air of calm could be felt, despite the sight of patients, some just children, walking around in their gowns and trundling their stands with dangling bottles of chemo along with them.

213

The actual treatment itself was a little nerve racking to start with. I lay down on a bed while above me was a big tubular piece of equipment which – once I had been correctly placed by the radiotherapist who then rather alarmingly beat a hasty retreat behind a sheet of glass – began to rotate above and around a strip of light onto my operation site as I held my arm above my head. It did not last for long and afterwards I was free to sit in the lounge and drink a glass or two of fruit juice.

I also had several sessions with a counsellor to whom I was able to express my dismay at this development. She explained that there seemed to be some correlation between a positive outlook and a good outcome, and she encouraged me to gather strength and to look forward and believe that all would be well. In addition, probably as part of the research, from time to time I was sent to the hospital photographer to have photos taken of my breasts, my face not included I hasten to add.

Towards the end of the six weeks of treatment I was feeling very tired, but perhaps because of my copious intake of fluids, I suffered only a very slight burning at the base of my throat. Eventually I went back to work and was prescribed Tamoxifen. Some years later a GP looked at my hospital records and told me that I had had a very low-grade growth which had been caught at a very early stage.

That Easter we went over to Majorca to spend some time there before I started picking up the reins at work again. We were sitting in the apartment on the evening of Good Friday when we heard the sound of singing and, looking out through the shutters, we saw a procession making its way along the new road around the Fort. At the head of it were three men carrying crucifixes and being chivvied along by others dressed as Roman soldiers. Crowded around them were people dressed in biblical robes and carrying torches. A long procession of ordinary people followed behind. We grabbed our coats as

214

a cold wind was blowing and hurried to join the back of the throng. They turned in through the gates in the archway into the Fort and climbed out onto the raised central area.

As the proceedings were all in Spanish we could not follow everything but it was obvious that the crucifixion of Christ and the two thieves was to be re-enacted. Despite the cold wind the gowns of the three men were taken off, they were tied to the crosses which were then set up in what must have been previously prepared holes in the rock. By then darkness had fallen and the whole scene became quite surreal as they hung there in the freezing wind while in the background, planes coming in to the airport shone their landing lights over us as they swept in to land just beyond us. Such a juxtaposition of ancient and modern, and yet both so relevant to the lives of us all and probably more particularly to me who had so recently been staring death in the face. To be honest, it was not so much the idea of death which worried me, but rather what the manner of it might be.

Returning to England we began to think long and hard about our future. Although I would not be completely out of the woods until at least five years had passed without a recurrence, the outlook was good and I was to have regular-check ups. This however, had been a wake up call and although, as a Crown servant rather than a civil servant, I would be entitled to stay on at work until the age of 65, I knew that was not what I wanted to do. We reckoned that by the time I was 60 and Alex was almost 65, we could perhaps count on at least ten good years before ill health or old age began to take its toll. It made sense, therefore, not to delay doing all that we might want to do.

Over the years Alex had often heard us talking about South Africa where the children had spent their childhoods, and where I had lived and worked both before and after the death of my first husband, Ron, the children's father. I knew that, along with my Crown Service pension I would receive

215

a lump sum. What better way to spend some of it than by taking a prolonged trip to South Africa? I still had a few contacts there, Ron's sisters Margery, a retired Salvation Army Officer, and younger sister Miriam and her husband Ron, all lived there still. Margery had a flat on the south coast of Natal at a place called Uvongo, and Miriam and Ronnie lived at Rosebank in Johannesburg. In addition, my nephew Bram and his wife Chrissie also lived in Johannesburg. They had stayed with us some years before when visiting England and were most keen for us to come and visit them.

By chance I saw an advertisement for flights to South Africa by a company called 'The Friends of the Springbok'. Intrigued, I sent off for some information. At that time South Africa, due to its system of apartheid, was the pariah of the world. Over the years I had refused to be drawn into talking about the time that I had spent there myself, as someone who had never visited the country could not possibly know what it had been like to live in that beautiful land during the 50s and 60s. Not many people living in England could possibly understand the difference in the cultures of people with a European heritage and those of African origin, whose backgrounds and centuries of living a simple hand to mouth existence had held sway for thousands of years, bolstered by a complicated tribal lifestyle. This could not have been demonstrated better than by a scheme set up by the prevailing British government in the late 1940s. No doubt not many people now recall what was called 'The Groundnut Scheme'. It was decided that in order to improve the living conditions of people in one of the central African states – I don't recall exactly which one it was – groundnuts, which produced peanuts, so I am told, would be cultivated and would provide a source of income for the residents of that land. Great trouble was taken to gather together the men of the far-flung villages and all was explained to them in great detail, but what the experts had failed to realise was that it was the

216

women who did all the cultivating, not the men, and the scheme died a death. As far as I know there may have been other factors working against the success of such a scheme, but it serves to demonstrate how easily assumptions are made by people with no knowledge of the African culture and way of life.

However a man called Stuart Weaving realised that there were many people whose sons and daughters had gone to live in South Africa and who might need help in arranging their flights. A remarkable and likeable Yorkshire man, his interest in the country had been triggered when he took the official Welsh rugby side and their supporters to South Africa in 1964. He found that there was a strong bond between many living there and people in England so he started a friendship travel service between the two countries. Politics held no interest for him, but people did. In a quote from his book *Ambassador of Friendship* he says:

It is not just a question of the colour of a person's skin. The disparate races have much in common, but also differ in social attitudes to a degree not always understood by those who have not been there or paid but fleeting visits.

His own opinion was that there was no easy solution to the problems of the country and that the best people to find a solution were the people of the country themselves. Meanwhile, isolation either in business or sport was at best unhelpful, and at worst did incalculable harm. From that standpoint, he did all in his power to foster sporting relationships between the two countries and to give assistance to those wishing to travel there.

Much of this I was to find out later, but in the meantime I responded to the advertisement and in due course received a bulging envelope containing much of the information we needed if we were to undertake a trip once we retired. Set out in magazine style with large readable print, it clearly spelt out the fares to Johannesburg, Durban or Cape Town and gave much more information besides. Of great interest to us was the fact that every other month or so a meeting was held in an hotel near Heathrow airport where 'Friends of the Springbok' could meet to watch a film of South Africa and to partake in the raffle of which the first prize was two return tickets to South Africa. From then on we went to practically every meeting where we met so many people keen to travel to that lovely land, although we never managed to win the raffle!

Over the years, when life had been so busy and I had moved from one challenge to another, I had given little thought to the years I had spent in South Africa. They had at times been wonderful and at other times there had been periods when I had sunk to the lowest ebb. The loss of my husband, leaving me with the care of a young family, had been a shattering experience from which I had had to climb out with great difficulty until finally accepting the fact that there was no longer a life for me in that lovely land. It was 22 years since I had arrived back in England with a few suitcases, four children and £50 in a building society in Newcastle. How much water had flowed under so many bridges since then! And yet the urge was there to return and to see once more the places I had known. And knowing the country so well, it would be an opportunity to travel in a way that, while I lived there, had not been possible.

20

Early in 1990 I let it be known that I would not be staying on after my 60th birthday in July of that year, giving the management time to set up boards to select my replacement. As the time grew closer I drew a little calendar and happily marked off each day as the year went on.

After attending the Trooping of the Colour in June there was little time left, so I began to make arrangements for my leaving 'do'. The House of Commons had a catering sub-committee offering banqueting services for formal occasions. As a lowly HEO these were not available to me, but my boss, as an Officer of the House, kindly sponsored me and I received a copy of the printed regulations, forms and prices. There were four terrace dining rooms to choose from and I selected the largest which could hold about 80 people standing. I had invitations printed for Friday 13th July, 1990 for 'Pat Lowther's Retirement Party' between 12.30 and 2.30 pm and ordered a finger buffet, 40 bottles of wine, fruit juices and sparkling water. As well as the people I worked with, all the family came and some of the people I had worked with at the West End office. It was a wonderful occasion and afterwards the family and I walked down Victoria Street to the station, loaded down with the flowers I had been given as well as several other lovely gifts.

July was very hot that year. Paul and Clara had come over from Majorca and Chris and Maggie down from Yorkshire, so on the Saturday we had another big party for the family at Meopham which my friend Jane helped me to cater for. The next day, my sixtieth birthday, the family left to return to their homes and we had another party for all our friends living round about us.

On the following Monday morning I awoke with the wonderful realisation that I did not have to get up, get ready and dash to the station to catch that flipping train! Working days were over and my time was all my own.

Before leaving the city I had taken the opportunity to visit the South African Tourist Board, or SATOUR as it was known, at their offices in Regent Street, and there I had picked up a selection of brochures in order to plan our trip. Knowing the country as I did, I knew exactly where I wanted us to go and such a trip could not be undertaken in less than three months. We would stay with my nephew Bram and his wife Chrissie in Johannesburg, and with my sister-in-law Margery in Uvongo in Natal. Occasionally we would use hotels, but I had found a brochure listing private homes where visitors stayed for bed and breakfast, and I rather liked the sound of that.

Anne had been having a bad time recently. A hysterectomy had gone wrong and she had had to be rushed back into theatre for a further operation to stem a haemorrhage, so it had taken her some time to recover. Knowing how much she often longed for South Africa, during the summer we had taken her with us to the Friendship meetings and so we asked her if she would like to accompany us at the start of our holiday, for a month perhaps. She felt she would have to ask Dave and rather reluctantly he said she could go but she would have to pay for herself. My blood boiled, after all she had been through, and he must have known that she had no money as she had had to give up her part-time job owing to her health problems. We decided we would pay for her, and she could repay us whatever she could afford afterwards. Even then, she did not feel she could leave her family for a month and was all for going just for two weeks, but eventually she agreed to three weeks.

The staff at the office at the Friendship House in Staines were most helpful in doing all the bookings of hotels and hiring of cars for the whole of the itinerary I had set out. We would spend three weeks in Johannesburg, during which time we would make a trip to the Kruger Park Game Reserve and the Northern Transvaal. After that, Anne would return to England and we would make our way down to the Natal coast and stay with Margery for three weeks. From there we would go along the coast through the Transkei to East London and Port Elizabeth, spending a week along the Garden Route through Plettenberg Bay and Knysna before arriving in Cape Town. After spending two weeks there we would drive up the centre of the country, to Kimberley and a three-day stay before returning to Johannesburg and spending a final three weeks with Bram and Chrissie.

So it was that on a brilliant autumn morning we loaded our cases into our car and drove through the beautiful Kent countryside to Croydon to pick up Anne. It was such a lovely morning that I almost felt I would rather stay in England. It seemed so strange to be returning to the country where so many things had happened. After all, it was twenty-two years ago, much had changed, the people I had known would have moved on. Events in South Africa had more or less passed me by, although I knew that there had been some slackening of the apartheid regime. Four years previously the pass laws had been abolished, leading to freedom of movement for the black population and in February of that year, Nelson Mandela had been freed. Nonetheless, there had been violence in the Townships just the previous month.

We had arranged to have our car stored at a facility near to Heathrow from where we would be ferried to the airport for the evening flight, so after picking Anne up we made our way there. The car would be under cover for the whole three months and would be far more secure than leaving it standing at Meopham where we did not have a garage. As

221

we were driven to the airport, the young man asked us where we were going and when we said South Africa he was speechless. We had to laugh, remarking that it was a real conversation stopper.

Arriving at the drop-off point we made our way to the check-in and, relieved of our cases, went to the nearby café where we had arranged to meet my nephew's wife, Louise, who was anxious to see us off. We had offered to look up her foster mother, but she was a bit evasive and did not seem very keen for us to do that. I understood that they were Afrikaans-speaking people with very little English and perhaps she felt they would be uncomfortable with us, so we did not press it.

Eventually our flight was called and we said our goodbyes and made our way to the departure lounge. We were lucky to be allocated seats in the upper deck of the jumbo jet and soon settled down for the night-time flight. During the night, somewhere over Africa, Anne and I were woken by some turbulence and we gazed out at an electric storm as lightning flicked among towering storm clouds. We slept again and woke to see the sun rising over the early morning mist clouds. Already England seemed far away both in memory and distance.

Soon we were approaching Jan Smuts Airport and I looked down once more on that runway that I had last seen as I took off with my family twenty-two years ago. It was hard to ignore the lump in my throat and a feeling of unshed tears. So much had happened over the intervening time and now I was returning to a place I had never expected to see again. The plane landed and taxied to a halt, and before long we were through all the controls and being greeted by Bram who had Railton and Timothy, his two older sons, with him.

There was little I recognised as we drove to his home in Constantia Kloof along wide new roads and past pleasant tree-lined suburbs. His house was built on a hillside and the huge gates opened into the grounds. We parked on the wide drive, while below us a lovely swimming pool sparkled in the early morning sunlight. Chrissie and youngest son Christopher waited to greet us, and we were shown to our rooms and soon settled in.

Thus began three weeks of pure delight. That night as we sat around the dinner table Bram asked me if I remembered people I had known all those years ago with whom I had not kept in touch. He suggested I might like to phone them, so we got out the phone book and sure enough, some of them were listed. The first were Cynthia and Val with whom we had travelled to South Africa by boat in the early 1950s. When Cynthia answered the phone she could hardly believe who it was that was calling, and after a lovely chat we agreed that we would arrange to meet up before we left Johannesburg.

Next were Hilda and Len Hickenbottom who had been our nextdoor neighbours when we had lived in a suburb called Bryanston and once more we promised to arrange to meet up. That was enough excitement for one day.

The next morning Bram took us into central Johannesburg to the Carlton Centre where up on the observation platform we had a panoramic view of the city and were able to pick out various landmarks. Then we drove around some of the southern suburbs where we had lived but which now seemed very down at heel. In the evening we had our first dip in the swimming pool although the water was still a bit cool.

The following Sunday, Anne, Alex and I drove to Johannesburg to attend the service at the Salvation Army where the family and I had worshipped so many years ago. Parking the car we climbed the steps to the entrance and were invited to sign the visitors book. Entering the hall, we took our seats near the centre, and as we settled in I heard a voice behind me whisperiing, 'It's Pat! I'm sure it's Pat!' Glancing round I recognised the wife of the Social Secretary who had been my boss and beside her, the couple who had been in charge of the Training College at the time I left South Africa. There was just time for a quick 'hallo' and handshake before the service began.

During the announcements the names of visitors were read out. I had put mine down as Pat Lowther, formerly Malone together with Alex's and Anne's names. As they were announced another shout went up from across the hall, 'It's Pat!' To say I was astonished was putting it mildly. After all, it was many years since I had left and I had not kept in touch with anyone, although I have no doubt Margery had probably reported my doings from time to time.

Once the meeting had closed, I was surrounded by so many people whom I had known. Alex was introduced and it was some time before the hall could be cleared as so many people wanted to talk. Anne, however, was a bit disappointed that many of the young people she had known no longer worshipped there.

Over the next day or two we visited the Krugersdorp area to the west of the city and the house we had lived in there. It was currently empty so we peered in through the windows and, amazingly, little seemed to have changed. We fitted in a trip to the Voortrekker Monument near Pretoria, and to Gold Reef City, an old gold mine which had been turned into a visitors' attraction with an opportunity to go down the mine shaft and to see gold being poured.

A trip out to Sun City, a casino and hotel complex built in the hills out beyond Magaliesberg, was a wonderful experience as the jacarandas were in bloom and the whole area was fresh with lawns, tropical plants, carp in pools and exotic birds wandering amid the paths and waterfalls. We had a flutter on the machines and I won 40 rand and Alex 150 rand, which paid for a splendid lunch at one of the many restaurants.

However, there was one more sombre visit which had to

be made and that was to the crematorium. It was a bit difficult to find as a new motorway was now running alongside and we could not see the entrance. I noticed Dove's, the funeral directors, at the roadside so we called in. They suggested we should leave the car with them for safety, and walk the short distance across the pedestrian foot bridge to the entrance gate.

I knew exactly where the plaque was and looked once more at the words I had chosen so many years ago:

IN MEMORY OF

RONALD MALONE

GOD'S SOLDIER.

BELOVED HUSBAND,

FATHER AND SON.

8.9.21–17.7.65

How much had changed in the twenty-five years since that plaque had been installed. How could I have envisaged what the future would hold on the day when Ron's coffin was carried down these paths accompanied by the Salvation Army band and crowds of fellow officers and friends. On that day the future had looked not just bleak but almost insurmountable, and yet day by day and month by month time had passed, decisions had been made, and now I stood in this spot twenty-five years later with our eldest daughter, herself the mother of three children and a husband to whom I had been married for longer than my first marriage had lasted.

Thoughtfully we made our way back to the car and drove across the town to see the little house we had lived in in Bez Valley and the Army Training College in Troyeville, now no longer being used as a college. The door was answered by a lady, an Envoy, who managed the place as a refuge for men in need of a place to stay. She invited us in and showed us around, where I found that much remained unchanged and it brought back memories of my college days. We decided that was enough strolling down memory lane for one day and drove back to Bram's to enjoy an evening in the garden.

The next day we set off early for a trip north to Warmbaths, about 60 miles from Johannesburg. Here, where hot springs bubbled up, a marvellous complex had been built. In the centre was a huge open-air pool which, when stepped into, felt like having a warm bath. (Hence the name, no doubt!) A helter-skelter had been built to one side giving an exciting ride through pools and rapids while on the far side, among fountains and tropical foliage, a large building held various treatment rooms and a remedial spa. We spent a lovely day dipping in the pool, sunbathing and relaxing before driving into the town to find a restaurant for dinner.

A few days later we returned our hire car and the next morning at 5.30 am Anne, Alex and I set off with Bram in his people carrier for the Kruger Park Game Reserve. It had rained through the night and the morning was cold and damp as we set off on the northern motorway towards Pretoria to pick up the western road towards the low veldt. Bram swung off the excellent surface of the N1 onto lesser roads through an area containing scattered Ndbele settlements but not a road sign to be seen. However, pressing westwards without seeing another car or person, we finally reached the N4 and thankfully stopped at a Golden Egg restaurant for a well-earned breakfast. As we reached a place called Waterfall Boven the rain clouds had lifted and we decided to call a halt and visit the waterfall that gave it its name. It was once a mining town, and the falls were reached along an unlit and unused railway tunnel through which we stumbled until at last we came out into daylight and were able to see the splendid falls. Sadly, the little town off to the other side of the main road was largely deserted.

Setting off once more we began the descent from the high

veldt down through the beautiful scenery of the Elands River Valley and as we turned north at Nelspruit, the sun was shining and the air was warm and humid. We had not booked a trip to the game reserve before we left England, deciding to leave it until we arrived and could see how it fitted in to our three-week itinerary in Johannesburg. Bram had phoned the reservations office for us and we had been lucky enough to get two nights' accommodation at a camp called Berg-en-Dal, situated at the very south of the reserve which itself is about the size of Wales. So the plan was to swing further north and enter the reserve at the Numbi Gate. Now in the late afternoon, we drove through miles of African settlements where the roads were crowded with youngsters coming home from school. Each house was set in a fair-sized plot of ground and I was surprised to notice that there was very little cultivation, the area being left as a beaten patch of earth with a few chickens scratching around under the scrub-like bushes, but here and there an occasional home seemed to be a cut above the rest.

At last we reached the Numbi Gate and checked in at the arrivals office. As we got out to stretch our legs we realised that now the heat was intense, so we were glad to climb back into the air-conditioned vehicle and make our way into the reserve. Leaving the main road and taking small side tracks, almost immediately we saw herds of impala, zebra and stately giraffe. Further on a troupe of baboons and monkeys played in the trees, but as the sun beat down upon us, overcoming the air-conditioned interior, we decided to head for our camp and call it a day after our exhausting drive.

After checking in we were directed to our guesthouse. Things had obviously moved on since my last visit to Kruger Park so many years ago with Ron and the children. Then we had stayed in a large rondavel with earthen floors and thatched roof, our beds and rough tables and chairs arranged around the room, while outside, fires were stoked up by the communal shower blocks and at night, under the stars, we cooked our meals on *braai*s, as the barbecues are called.

Now as we wended our way through the camp, we noted the restaurant, the well-stocked shop, and the place where we were to stay. This proved to be a splendid thatched and brick-built house. On entering, we found ourselves in a huge lounge/dining room with a fully equipped kitchen as part of the open-plan space. At the far side were sliding patio doors onto a private terrace with the ever-present *braai* facilities. The room itself was furnished with lovely cane furniture upholstered in material to match the full-length curtains. Through a door was a passage leading to a separate wing where there were two twin-bedded bedrooms for Bram and Anne, each with its own shower room with toilet and wash basin. On the other side was another twin-bedded suite with full en-suite bathroom and sliding door leading onto another private patio. Everything was spotless and Joseph, the house boy, welcomed us in and showed us where everything was. Such luxury! Later we found the guest book which was signed by Nelson Mandela and Winnie as well as the prime minister, Mr de Klerk. We could only think that with our last-minute booking, this had been all that was available, but with the excellent exchange rate we could well afford it.

After settling in, we strolled over to see what was on offer in the shop. While there was not a huge selection, we bought sufficient supplies for a *braaivleis* the next evening. After checking out the restaurant we returned to our thatched cottage for showers and, freshened up, then went back to the restaurant's air-conditioned comfort. We enjoyed a three-course meal, well prepared and beautifully served, after which coffee was taken in the comfortable lounge. No roughing it here then! Additionally the cost was reasonable at R21 per head, which amounted to just over £5 each.

As darkness fell we walked to the square where, seated

in a stepped amphitheatre, we watched a wildlife film about hippos and crocodiles. Back at our guesthouse we settled in for the night, to be ready for an early start next day.

Leaving the camp at 5 am, just as the gates were opened, we drove around for an hour or two, but there was little to be seen so we came back and had a good breakfast. As this camp was at the southernmost tip of the reserve, game was usually sparse as it was far from some of the watering places. So after we had eaten we set out once more towards Skukuza, arriving in the early afternoon. After watching the weaver birds in the trees hanging over the river and some lazy crocodiles on its banks, we set off once more, making for the Sabie River.

We turned in to a loop which overlooked the river, and gazed across the thick vegetation. What I had thought was a big grey rock suddenly started to move. It was an elephant! Soon the crashing noises heralded the arrival of several more, but then they disappeared from view. On our way back to our base camp, however, we came across them again. Several cars had stopped as the herd crossed the road, too many to count and with one baby sheltering beneath its mother's enormous legs.

That evening we enjoyed our *braai* outside in the warm darkness before moving inside for a nightcap. Suddenly, beyond the closed patio doors, we saw some movement outside. It was a little genet (a small rodent-like creature with bright eyes, dark spots on it's fur and a long ringed tail) hunting for scraps! We obligingly put out some of the bones from our meal, which it promptly picked up and scurried off into the bush with. This was our last night at Berg-en-Dal, so we retired early ready to set off quickly the next day.

We were leaving the game reserve at a gate further north to stay for a night at a place called the Swadini Rest Camp in a valley near the Blyde River Canyon, but we intended to spend the day travelling up through the game reserve for a last chance to see what we could. Our decision paid off as, travelling along a road alongside a dried-out riverbed, many cars had stopped. We were just in time to see lion strolling among them before moving down onto the river bed, where a whole pride of them walked nonchalantly and majestically away beyond our sight on the other side of the slope.

Pressing on, we came to a rest stop where we were able to leave our vehicle and stroll to the toilets on the far side of the lightly wooded area. Suddenly, we heard a voice calling, 'Anne! Anne!' Not imagining for a moment that anyone would be calling my daughter, we walked on, until a figure came rushing towards us. It was one of Anne's erstwhile South African friends whom she had caught up with when we visited the Army a few Sundays before, and who was now also on a trip to the game reserve. Talk about a Stanley and Livingston moment! It was lovely to see her and we enjoyed a chat before moving on again.

After leaving the game reserve, we found the Swadini Rest Camp nestled in a valley. It also lived up to our expectations. We had a spacious chalet set in a large lawned area beneath towering crags. The floors were tiled, the ceilings were all of pine and the well-equipped kitchen had a microwave and large fridge-freezer. This was just to be an overnight stop before moving on but we were more than comfortable. There was time to have a quick early morning swim in the outdoor pool the next day while baboons paced solemnly around the grounds. Warning notices against feeding or approaching them were everywhere, as they could be vicious.

Leaving at 8.30 while it was still cool, we set off to see the Blyde River Dam before taking a winding 160-km road up and through the mountains to the very top. As the crow flies, we had only travelled 8 km. Driving through a tunnel cut into the hills, we finally reached the viewpoint from which was spread out a wonderful panorama of three peaks on a distant slope. It resembled nothing more than three gigantic rondavels, which of course was how it had earned its name, The Three Rondavels. The air was clear, making a striking sight as, caught in the sunlight, the peaks stood out from the dark shadows behind.

From there we drove to a spot called Bourkes Luck Potholes, where the river had gouged out a weird succession of holes in the rock, then on to the Berlin falls, where we were the only visitors. Our final stop was at a place called God's Window, where after struggling up a rutted pathway we suddenly came upon a vista stretching far across the game reserve and over into Mozambique, a place currently torn by civil war.

A quick visit to Pilgrim's Rest proved to be a bit disappointing, but its importance lay in having been the first place where gold had been discovered in the 1870s. For a brief time it had swarmed with prospectors from around the world, but now it drowsed in the low veldt heat, as it had soon been found that the gold trickling down in the streams was actually the residue from the massive gold fields up on the high veldt.

Time was passing so we pressed on back up north to Tzaneen and up into the hills again, heading for the Magoebaskloof Hotel. Magoebaskloof (pronounced Ma-hoo-bas-kloof) was set among the hills and forests, and in times gone by had been the reputed haunt of the Rain Queen. One could almost believe it when seeing the mists drift in and out of the valleys and hearing the chuckle of streams rapidly descending to the plains below.

For Anne this was to be the highlight of our trip. Many years ago, when we had been living over here, I had sent both Paul and Anne to board at a rural school among these beautiful hills. My late husband's alcoholism had been at its peak and I wanted the children to be where they could not witness his behaviour. I had seen a newspaper article about these rural schools which needed more pupils in order to keep them going and it seemed like the ideal solution. My aunt Ethel was visiting us, so we made the journey up here and stayed at the Magoebaskloof Hotel. At that time it was a rather rundown place, but situated at the head of an enormous valley, it had splendid views from the rooms at the back. We had inspected the school and found it to be all we wished for and so the two children had spent some time there before I was able to bring them back home. Anne had many happy memories of the school and of the area. Now, not only were we going to revisit the school, we were also staying at the hotel for one night.

Things had certainly moved on since we were last here. The place was now a five-star hotel and, while retaining much of the old-world charm, it had been transformed into an upmarket hostelry obviously patronised by the great and the good. We were welcomed at the desk by an African receptionist whose splendid physique was matched by his personal charm. Settling in to our rooms I found that the open balconies of yore had been enclosed and the whole wall filled in with windows which gave out on to the view which I remembered so well. I drank my fill of it before having a restorative shower, then meeting the others for dinner.

Next morning, after a breakfast which we made the most of, we left and took the road to Haenertsburg, the small village where the school was. They were most kind and let us wander around the grounds and the premises as the school was closed for half term. Then we went back to the village and visited the tiny Anglican church which the children used to attend each Sunday. Sadly it was closed, with a notice on the door saying that services were held once a month.

Setting off once more we drove straight back to Johannesburg, arriving in the early afternoon. We had driven

2,200 km. The next day we visited the Hyperama Shopping Centre and Anne bought gifts to take home. We spent the day quietly, as on the morrow Anne was flying back to England. After packing up next morning we loaded the car and Bram took us to a place called The Courier for lunch. It was an outdoors affair under a pergola with lambs roasting on a spit, while in an adjoining room we were invited to go and help ourselves at a table groaning under the weight of hors d'oeuvres of meats, fish, salmon, eggs, prawns and salads. This was followed by a course of roast meats and vegetables, and all the while we were entertained to a selection of music played on the piano. Really, I tend to run out of superlatives!

After sweet and coffee we left for the airport where Anne was just in time for check-in. It had been a wonderful holiday for her, and for us too, one that none of us would ever forget. But for us this was only the start, as the next day we also packed up and loading up our hire car, set off on the N3 towards Durban. We spent a couple of nights at an hotel in the Drakensberg called the Sandford Park Lodge, but as Alex wasn't feeling too well we rested quietly before moving on again under grey skies and light rain. Bypassing Durban, we found the south coast road and made our way to Uvongo and a warm welcome from Margery, my late husband's sister.

21

We spent the next three weeks with Margery in her flat at Uvongo. It was a very nice block, three storeys high, and Marge was on the first floor. Her flat had two large bedrooms and a big lounge with a wall of windows looking out onto the lawns sloping down to a small secondary road and a very brief glimpse of the sea. She was renting the property having sold her house at St Michaels on Sea a little further down the coast, after her husband Bram had died three or four years before. She had spent some of the money on a new car and given a sizeable lump to her son, Bram, up in Johannesburg to help him buy his house. The rest she invested in a local building society paying a good rate of interest and she lived quite well on her Salvation Army pension and a small South African pension. Her UK pension was paid into a bank in England where she allowed it to accumulate, flying over from time to time to have a spending spree at Marks and Spencer.

However, fate had caught up with her in the guise of the new owners of the block of flats. The original owner had died and his son had inherited the property which, up until then, had been protected by a covenant giving security of tenure to the tenants. The son had now gone to court and had been able to break the covenant, and all were under notice to vacate unless they wished to buy at a preferential rate. Margery had written to tell us this before we left England, so Alex and I had had time to discuss the matter. As we had money lying on deposit, we had decided that if the property seemed to be a good investment, we would buy it on Margery's behalf and charge her an economical rent. We were quite impressed with the flat and so decided to go ahead.

Meanwhile we got to know the area. The South Coast, as it was popularly known, encompassed a long stretch of the coastline from Durban all the way to Port Edward, the last place before the Transkei. This was a huge tract of land running all the way to East London and run by the Africans with its capital and seat of government at Umtata. The most popular area of the South Coast was the short stretch from Port Shepstone, quite a large town containing the local government offices, down to Ramsgate and Margate, with Uvongo somewhere in the middle. The area was the holiday venue of choice for the bulk of people living up in Johannesburg, and during the holiday periods, the shops and restaurants, to say nothing of the beaches, would be packed with visitors. Consequently, this was also an area where many Transvaal folk chose to retire, so there were few people who had actually been born and bred there, but many now enjoyed their sunset years in such a choice location. With lush tropical vegetation, long stretches of golden sands and brilliant blue sea, what was there not to like? We were delighted, especially when we were welcomed so warmly everywhere we went. We attended the local Methodist Church where Margery did the sick-visiting, and met many of her friends. Invitations flooded in and we were entertained to tea in many of the local homes.

There were several large shopping centres with air-conditioned comfort and a choice of cafés and restaurants up and down the coast. We soon discovered how reasonable the property prices were, not only when set against our exchange rate but also when we discovered that a specially good rate was on offer to settlers who came and brought their pounds with them. For instance, a four-bedroomed house with double garage and two bathrooms was on sale for

235

R130,000 or approximately £25,000, while interest rates at the banks and building societies were between 15 and 18 per cent.

After discussing it with Margery, we made the decision to buy her flat for her, although the rental she said she could afford was not as much as I would have expected. Still I decided she was Ron's sister and I was sure it was what he would have wanted me to do for her. We were also able to open an account at the building society that Marge used, so we deposited our traveller's cheques and were given debit cards to use at any cash machine, which was a relief from the safety aspect. Also, Margery would be able to deposit her rent into the same account once all the technicalities had been sorted out.

We made one trip away, taking Marge with us. This was to a tourist attraction many miles north of Durban in the depths of Natal, called Shakaland. There we stayed for a couple of nights in a beehive hut – with all mod. cons of course. We were introduced to Zulu life and culture. Freddie, an English-speaking Zulu, in telling us the history of his people, said that they originated in the sub-Sahara in the 1500s and over a hundred years or more gradually migrated south, displacing the little bushmen as they went, until finally they reached Zimbabwe and Southern Africa where they spit up into the Zulu, Xhosa and Nbledi tribes.

I was enthralled by the lifestyle in South Africa and by the manner in which we could improve our standard of living, to say nothing of the attraction of being able to buy a beautiful home. Alex knew how much I was tempted. At last, he admitted that for him, too, it seemed to be a dream come true, and more than we could have wished for in our wildest dreams. So when we left the South Coast in the middle of November, it was with the very clear idea of what we would like to do. Leaving a local solicitor to start the process of buying Marge's flat, we set off to drive through the Transkie to East London where, after an overnight stop, we would press on to Port Elizabeth, then down along the Garden Route.

At Port Elizabeth we met up with friends of my nephew, young Stephen, and spent a pleasant time with them. Undine and Aleck were actually in our age group, but had looked after Stephen some years ago when he was an apprentice in the telecommunications industry. His parents, Marge and Bram, who had been stationed there, had been moved on by the Army so he had lodged with Undine and Aleck while he had continued his training. They had looked on him as another son in addition to their own large family.

We had met them when they had been on a visit to the UK and Stephen had brought them to visit us at Meopham. It was great to see them again. They entertained us in their lovely home and showed us around some of the places of interest. At one point we passed a wooded area dotted with little shacks in the shape of wigwams. Aleck drew the car up nearby and we walked carefully near where we could see young boys covered in a white chalk-like substance carrying what looked like small bows and arrows and short wooden spears. Aleck explained that they were young African boys who, after their circumcision, were initiated into the tribe by proving that they could exist all alone in the bush. They were smeared with white clay to denote their status. We quietly moved away so as not to disturb their privacy.

We also paid a visit to Chrissie's mother, who lived in Port Elizabeth, and met one of her sisters and a brother. After a couple of nights we pressed on and visited the Tsitsikamma forest to see an 800-year-old yellow-wood tree. Leaving Port Elizabeth, our plan was to work our way along the coastline, known as the Garden Route, very aptly named as we were to enjoy lovely scenery, splendid vistas and magnificent horizons.

At our first stop, Plettenburg Bay, we stayed in a private

home on a bed and breakfast basis, a lovely house overlooking the bay and Beacon Island. Once a whaling station, this had been transformed into a stylish and upmarket hotel. A stupendous view could be seen through the rolled-back windows of the veranda running along the whole width at the back. The house itself was full of polished wood furniture, a great collection of copper utensils and gleaming polished wood floors. Beneath the veranda on the lower level was a suite of interconnected rooms consisting of bedroom, sitting room and bathroom with a door leading out onto the terraced lawn, which was our B&B accommodation.

We settled in, I made some tea and we took it out onto the garden, where Wendy our hostess joined us. Later we went out for a meal at a local restaurant and that night slept like logs. The next day we backtracked to some of the places we had passed the day before. The Stormsriver Mouth, a national park with a restaurant and café overlooking the sea, was spectacular and as we drank our coffee we watched the waves crashing onto the shore. That evening we sat and chatted to Wendy, and it transpired that she had known a distant employer of mine called S.G. Norman. I had worked in the office of his plumbing business many years ago. What a small world, and yet in South Africa not really unusual, as it often transpires that everyone has some link with everyone else!

Next day we carried on south to visit Knysna where the sea crashes through a large fault in the cliffs called The Heads to fill the huge lagoon on which the town is built. We found our next B&B at Wilderness, in a lovely spot outside the town, and spent a day at Knysna at Belvedere where, reputedly, the illegitimate son of George III, George Rex, had lived after serving some time as the Governor of the Cape Province. His family had now died out and the area had been developed as a retirement complex with Victorian-style cottages. We completed the day with a visit to Oudtshorn, the Cango Caves and an ostrich farm, as well as a crocodile and cat farm, where cheetahs, jaguars, leopards and lions were all sadly kept in captivity.

Pushing on, we called in at Mossel Bay to see The Post Office Tree, still standing after so many years. Here the old sailing ships would call in to take on fresh water in the days before the Cape Colony was established, and to leave mail to be picked up by the next ship going in the opposite direction.

We were fast approaching Cape Town and soon were looking down on False Bay from the Sir Lowrie Pass. From there we were able to avoid the city and, taking the coastal road, passed through Muizenberg, reaching Fish Hoek in the late afternoon.

It was now late in November and we had been on the road for ten days. We were staying at the Salvation Army guesthouse situated on the bay at Fish Hoek, some miles outside Cape Town, so we made good use of the next two weeks we spent there, visiting as many of the attractions as we could including a trip on the cable car up Table Mountain.

The officers who were running the guesthouse were old friends of mine who had been in training with Ron in the late 1940s. Their daughter and her husband were Army Officers in Harare, the erstwhile Salisbury, capital of the newly named Zimbabwe. I was astonished to discover that they had come with a long list of goods which were unobtainable in Harare, to buy both for themselves and for several friends. There were things as simple as reels of sewing cotton, material and paper patterns for a bride-to-be, as well as several small kitchen utensils and other items one might have expected to be readily available. Obviously, things were not going too well now that Ian Smith had been forced to hand over the country to Robert Mugabe. Fortunately we were not to know that this was merely the thin end of a very large wedge, which in years to come would become headline news.

While we were there, much drama was happening back at home as Margaret Thatcher was deposed and on November 28th we heard that John Major had taken over. No one we spoke to could understand why she had had to go, as she was held in very high esteem by people in South Africa.

Cape Town is lovely, but somehow I did not feel as much at home there as I had in Johannesburg or on the South Coast, so I was not sorry when we set off north once more, this time to make a stop at Kimberley on our way back to Johannesburg. Setting off just before 6 am we drove through the deserted city just as the sun was rising and after a last look at Table Mountain, we reached the N1 motorway and headed north. Stopping for breakfast after we had cleared the built-up areas, we bought fruit and cold drinks for the rest of the journey and set off through the hills of the Western Cape until we branched off onto the N12 for the long drive through the Great Karoo.

This semi-arid region with bone-dry air, intense sunshine and minimal rainfall has a harsh beauty of its own. The excellent road stretched ahead to a far horizon which, when reached, opened up to another long stretch of road and another horizon. We sped along though, at a good speed, and were thankful for the air-conditioned car. Once we saw an ostrich standing all alone at the side of the road, and in the occasional tree weaver birds were busy in their dangling nests.

We drove all day, reaching Kimberley about 4 pm and thankfully checked into our hotel. Our room was spacious and well furnished but as we stepped out of the car we noticed the change in the temperature in comparison to the Cape, from sunshine offset by bracing winds, to intense dry and airless heat. After freshening up we had a quick look around the town to check out how to reach the Big Hole the next day, bought a take-away meal and went back to our hotel for a well-earned rest.

Situated as it is on the edge of the desert, it seems an

unlikely place to build a town, but of course the reason lies in the discovery of diamonds, first of all by a young boy called Daniel Jacobs who lived on his father's farm. Collecting stones to play a game called 'five stones' with his sister, he noticed one glittering on the ground, but it was not until a visitor to the farm, probably realising what it was, admired it and was given it by the child that the discovery was made. This man later exchanged it for an even bigger stone which was called The Star of South Africa, while the original discovery weighed $21^1/4$ carats and was called The Eureka. Sadly, the family on whose farm it was found never got a penny.

Once the discovery was made, prospectors from around the world converged on the site and fortunes were made and lost overnight. The usual campsite grew up, which largely explained why the streets of Kimberley are so tortuous, as no one took overall control and set the place out in a grid, as had been done in Johannesburg. The prospectors would buy a licence to dig in a marked-out piece of ground over a huge area. After a time, some holes had gone down further than others, and systems of pulleys and ladders were needed to haul up the ore, so before long a deepening hole emerged. This, of course, became The Big Hole. To stand at its edge is to appreciate just how enormous it is. It is filled with deep-green water, while on the far side the silhouettes of the buildings of the town itself look like a child's set of bricks.

Beside the Hole, a small town has been built consisting of replicas of the buildings in the previous century. Among them is an undertakers, complete with coffins and choice of shrouds and a grieving widow in black sitting in the Chapel of Rest. At the other end of the scale, shouts and raucous music are heard at The Diggers Rest. A pawnbroker, newspaper office, billiard room, library, auctioneer, ballroom, church and a blacksmith complete the scenario. I was fascinated by the display of photos from that era, where bedraggled men laboured under the hot sun. Much of what they earned had to be spent on the water carriers who, due to the lack of local rivers and streams, brought that precious commodity many miles to the thirsty prospectors.

Before we left the town we went to visit the Bulfontein Diamond Mine. I had visited it many years ago when I had lived in Johannesburg. At that time the African miners lived in compounds on the premises, only leaving when they returned to their homes in various parts of the African continent at the end of their term of employment. Now, all was changed and the workers lived in the nearby townships. The threat of IDB, or Illegal Diamond Buying, was still in evidence as our group in the conducted tour were ushered into a large building to change from our sandals into very solid heavy shoes and a hard hat. We were each issued with an identity card to operate the security doors and gates as we entered the mine grounds. After a talk on Kimberley and the background to the mining industry, we watched a video before being taken by bus to the extraction plant. I remembered this from my previous visit, but as we were driven through the extensive grounds, I saw that the building shaped like a wigwam, which used to be the miners' chapel, was being demolished. Otherwise, the process remained the same and we watched the huge rollers which crushed the ore, until the final greased one picked up the diamonds.

Once back in the car we set off for Johannesburg, but when we were some miles away we had to pull to the side of the road as a thunderstorm hammered our car and torrential rain swept down the road.

We arrived back at Bram and Chrissie's in time to help them celebrate their nineteenth wedding anniversary with a splendid meal at a local restaurant. A couple of days later Marge flew up from the South Coast and we spent our final three weeks with them. I was able to catch up with some of my old friends and we enjoyed many lazy hours by the pool. Margery's Christmas shopping went on at a snail's pace, as a visit to a shopping mall usually resulted in the purchase of one gift at a time, meaning another trip was required the next day. Sometimes we managed to duck out of these trips, as we really did not want to spend our last few days trailing round shops.

We loved the bright, clear and cool Transvaal mornings, and relaxed and sunbathed until the afternoon heat and inevitable thunderstorm built up, after which the warm evenings with their early sunsets were ideal times to sit out on the decking and enjoy an evening meal outdoors.

Christmas Day came, with the three boys up early to open their piles of presents. We gave them money as we had no idea what they wanted and they were delighted with the gift. We would be leaving the following week. On New Year's Eve Marge went to bed early. Bram and Chrissie had gone to a party, so just before 12 o'clock Alex went to look for the boys. Only Railton, the eldest, was still awake, so the three of us went out to the back of the house to the rails at the end of the lawn. To the left of us the view was hidden by trees, and to the right we could see houses perched high above us on the rocky outcrop, while far below, with a full moon and a clear sky, we could see the street lights and cars moving between them as midnight approached. Suddenly fireworks were let off, rockets climbed into the sky as bells rang and cars sounded their hooters. In the still air we could make out the shouts of people below as they called out 'Happy New Year!' and then the church bells began to ring. The three of us hugged and wished each other all good things for the coming year.

I lingered as the others went inside. It was now 1991. What would the new year hold for us?. We had made up our minds to sell up and come back to live in this lovely vibrant country of South Africa where we felt so much at home, but many obstacles would have to be overcome. It

243

was hard not to look back over the last twenty-two years. In my mind's eye, I could see once more that evening in Johannesburg, as Christopher, Cathleen and I struggled through the airport loaded down with as much hand luggage as we could carry. Then, as our plane took off, I had not thought that I would return to this land, and our future was uncertain.

Now it seemed that my life had come full circle. Having left with so little, and after a chaotic start, I had returned after all this time with some wonderful experiences behind me; I had met some wonderful people and made many friends. Not only that, my family had all achieved adulthood and most of them were married with children of their own. I was a grandmother several times over and I was better off financially than I had ever been. And now, because of that, Alex and I had choices we could make about our future.

My chosen path in the civil service had been interesting and varied, culminating in my time at the House of Commons. And of course, best of all, Alex and I had met and married, and worked hard together to make a life for ourselves.

However, I had no doubts that we would eventually come back and settle here in South Africa, but we would have to be patient and take it one step at a time. The future beckoned us with lots of promise, as I happily went indoors and settled down for the night. Best of all, there was no doubt in my mind that, for me, life had certainly begun at forty.